Aiming at Maturity

Aiming at Maturity

The Goal of the Christian Life

S<small>TEPHEN</small> W. R<small>ANKIN</small>

CASCADE *Books* · Eugene, Oregon

AIMING AT MATURITY
The Goal of the Christian Life

Cascade Books
An Imprint of Wipf and Stock Publishers
199 W. 8th Ave., Suite 3
Eugene, OR 97401

www.wipfandstock.com

ISBN 13: 978-1-61097-246-8

Cataloging-in-Publication data:

Rankin, Stephen W.

    Aiming at maturity : the goal of the Christian life / Stephen W. Rankin.

    viii + 180 p. ; 23 cm. — Includes bibliographical references.

    ISBN 13: 978-1-61097-246-8

    1. Cristian Life. 2. Virtues. I. Title.

BV4501.2 .R32 2011

Manufactured in the U.S.A.

Contents

Acknowledgments

It is always a risky venture to do an adequate job of thanking people who help an author write a book. I start with colleagues, friends, and students (some who have become colleagues and friends) at Southwestern College in Winfield, Kansas, where I spent fourteen rewarding years as professor and campus minister. Many fruitful conversations helped enrich my thinking about major themes. Thanks as well to members of the Wesleyan Theological Society and the Wesleyan-Pentecostal Consultation. My gratitude goes also to the Kansas Christian Ashram and to a number of Sunday school classes in Kansas and Texas who invited me to try out some ideas in this work.

Certain persons deserve special thanks. The Rev. Dr. Bruce Baxter gave strong encouragement to an early concept around which this book is formed and was the first to suggest that maybe I had something worth publishing. Dr. Judy Henneberger and Ms. Betty McHone, colleagues in the Chaplain's Office at Southern Methodist University, read parts of the manuscript, but, more importantly, gave constant encouragement and picked up administrative slack so that I could concentrate on writing. Mr. Chad Scruggs also read parts of the work and made helpful comments. Dr. Peter Moore helped ferret out remaining typographical errors and call out my egregious use of the words "mere" and "merely." Because of his keen eye, readers will not have to endure that annoyance.

Finally, I want to say thank you to my spouse, Joni, who read the whole thing—more than once—and offered a number of helpful observations. Thanks also to my son, Abram, who carried the load in the first round of copyediting. Luke, Leah, and Aaron, your turn is coming.

Introduction
Searching for a Grown-Up Faith

Maybe there is a Peter Pan syndrome after all. You know the character, that mischievous, magical boy who lives in "Neverland" and refuses to grow up? Generations have loved the story, but it seems too much these days that people actually resist growing up.[1]

Consider this example: just prior to the release of the film *Grown Ups*, the stars of the show—Adam Sandler and his buddies Kevin James, David Spade, Rob Schneider, and Chris Rock—did a number of television interviews to promote it. The movie portrays a group of boyhood church league basketball teammates who get together after thirty years for the funeral of their old coach. I watched with fascination how the actors promoted this film. Interviewers constantly quizzed these now-in-their-40s men about what it's like to grow up, and they kept insisting that they resist the label even though all but Spade are married and some have children. What is so bad about growing up? The tone of their comments wasn't just about growing old. It was about growing up, about assuming adult responsibilities and losing the freedoms and fun of the adolescent years.

Television and movie comedies have long poked fun at people's foibles, but for a good while we've been "entertained" by grownups acting like children. We have traded Archie Bunker, the bigot, for the boys and girls on *Friends* (I know, this is an old one) and Tripp in *Failure to*

---

1. Dan Kiley is regarded as having coined the term "Peter Pan Syndrome" in his book *The Peter Pan Syndrome*.

1

Launch.[2] I wince when I hear a college girl[3] say, "My mom is my best friend," then I see Mom and she is dressed just like her twenty-year-old daughter. I know I'm meddling, but I think it is time we paid attention. These things tell us something about ourselves. Maybe there is a Peter Pan Syndrome.

Yet, while our society demonstrates resistance to growing up, in truth we all aspire to it. Recall how you felt when you came of age and got that drivers license. The right to vote marks another desirable sign of adulthood. Most obvious of all for those of us who work in higher education, the main purpose of going to college is to get ready for adult life, and students are supposed to start practicing as soon as they hit campus. I witness this hunger-to-grow phenomenon every day. Yes, college students are notorious for partying and bad behavior, but they also have a vision of their better selves that they are determinedly trying to live into. Not all engage in the stereotypical party scene, and even most of those who do soon grow tired of the excess (and danger). They begin to recognize the shortsightedness of many of the goals they had when they first arrived on campus. They want to—and the overwhelming majority will—become contributing members of adult society. Eventually.

But what does adult society offer them if, once they join us, they find that we have not grown up ourselves? This question challenges Christians (especially us older ones) to face ourselves squarely. When young people look at us, searching for role models and mentors, what do they see?

I am aiming this book, therefore, at older or more experienced Christians, so to speak, but I'm writing with young people in mind. (I hope some of them will want to read it, too.) Do they find wise guides whom they can follow into a grown-up version of Christian discipleship? Apparently not. We seem to have lost track of what being a grown-up Christian looks like. Researchers in the Barna Group have discovered via phone interviews that neither lay Christians nor professional clergy

---

2. Matthew McConaughey plays Tripp in a movie that the IMDB summarizes as "a thirtysomething slacker suspects his parents of setting him up with his dream girl so he'll finally vacate their home." See online: www.imdb.com/title/tt0427229.

3. I know it's not *au courant* to call college women "girls," but they often use the term for themselves. Among the college men I work with, I constantly hear them refer to each other as "kids." No kidding.

can give an adequate description of spiritual maturity. In fact, "Most Christians equate spiritual maturity with following the rules."[4]

This gap has produced unfortunate results in society at large, but we can see its impact particularly in the spiritual lives of young people. Like the miners of old who kept one eye on the canary in the mineshaft, we can learn something by listening to young people. Christian Smith is among those scholars doing work on this topic. A number of important books have come from this research, two of which I will mention here. The first, *Soul Searching: The Religious and Spiritual Lives of American Teenagers* (Oxford University Press, 2005), sheds light on what 13 to 17 year olds think about faith and spirituality. Warning: Smith includes kids who think of themselves as *active and sincere Christians*. After listening to hundreds of interviews, Smith concludes: "A specific, important impediment to making sense of adolescent life in the United States . . . is the *routine failure of adults to recognize the responsibility of their own adult world, into which youth are being socialized.* Instead of owning this responsibility, however, adults typically frame adolescence in ways defining teenage life per se *as itself* a social problem."[5] Did we catch it? Let me put it bluntly: teenagers and emerging adults are the way they are because we adults are the way we are.[6]

From the follow-up work, *Souls in Transition: The Religious and Spiritual Lives of Emerging Adults* (Oxford University Press, 2009), we get a picture of the same teenagers now as 18 to 23 year olds.[7] Again, the description is stark: "Emerging adults struggle earnestly to establish themselves as autonomous and sovereign individuals. But the crises of knowledge and value that have so powerfully formed their lives leaves them lacking in conviction or direction to even know what to do with

4. Barna Group, "Many Churchgoers and Faith Leaders Struggle to Define Spiritual Maturity."

5. Smith, *Soul Searching*, 262. Emphasis added.

6. See also Dean, *Almost Christian*. This book was not yet in print as I finished the current work.

7. The term "emerging adults" has become fairly common among people who work with young people in their college years. By their own self-descriptions, young people in college or at college-age do not think of themselves as fully adult, the way earlier generations have done at age eighteen or twenty-one. But neither are these young people "adolescents." The term "emerging adults" gives a name to the prolonged and fluid entrance into adulthood, a phenomenon that we are currently witnessing.

their prized sovereignty."[8] What social forces helped produce the crises of knowledge? A paradox emerges here. On the one hand, young people rather fiercely protect their prerogatives (Smith's comment about autonomous individuals), yet they also easily share of their hunger for significant relationships with mentors who offer the wisdom that, for the most part, only more experienced exemplars can offer. Where are those exemplars?

All that I have said so far points to the crying need for a renewed focus on spiritual maturity. We need to know what it is and how we aim at it. That is the whole purpose of this book.

WHAT SPIRITUAL MATURITY ISN'T

In order to explore what spiritual maturity is, we need first to clarify what it is not. Spiritual maturity cannot be reduced to any of the following common descriptions, even though each offers a glimpse of something good and valuable. Keeping in mind that each point below contains a measure of truth, we still recognize that spiritual maturity is not:

1. *Mere adherence to rules.* Here we return to the problem the Barna Group has spotted. Following rules easily gives a false sense of success, even superiority toward those deemed not to have followed the rules. Furthermore, we lose sight of how easily we rationalize how well we follow rules. Finally, such an emphasis on rule following directs attention almost exclusively to the external, outward, and formal while ignoring the heart.

2. *Extensive Bible knowledge.* One can be good at intellectually grasping vast quantities of biblical material and drawing interesting and even true conclusions, but we dare not equate mere content knowledge with spiritual maturity. Knowledge understood this way actually has more to do with the mere manipulation of concepts. It is a speculative knowledge that, again, can tempt us toward a feeling of superiority rather than humble service. The point of knowing the Word is to do the Word. As the book of James has it, we're not to be forgetful hearers but effectual doers.

3. *Academic knowledge of theology or doctrine.* Likewise with this one. The ability to master complex theological ideas and build doctrinal systems does not automatically translate to the character of Christ

8. Smith, *Soul Searching*, 294.

embodied in our lives.[9]

4. *Regularity in religious activities.* For whatever reason, some people love the church culture: attending Sunday worship, joining in fellowship activities, participating in a small group or even a mission effort—and doing so with a high degree of regularity. Clearly, religious activity does not automatically produce spiritual growth.

I would guess that most people looking at this list would readily agree that its content does not necessarily produce a grown-up faith. Then why—to go back to the Barna Group's discovery—do so many people equate spiritual maturity with following the rules? What has happened? Ironically, the answer lies in that far too many of us have stopped paying attention to the Scriptures dealing expressly with spiritual maturity.

A GROWN-UP FAITH

To help improve the situation, we need to reclaim this vision: the goal for every Christian should be to become spiritually mature—to become a grown-up disciple. This book attempts to impart that vision and to offer some ways in which we can tell whether we are aiming at the goal.

First, however, I must share my ambivalence over terms. In writing this book, I have struggled with using words like *mature* and *maturity* to refer to this central, crucial goal of Christian discipleship. These days, the word *mature* suggests "old," and we Americans generally exhibit an allergic reaction to "old." I was born in the middle of the baby boom and I am exceedingly aware of how television advertisements market certain experiences to help my generation stay young and active as we go kicking and screaming toward the senior years. One of the most egregious shows a gray-haired but youthful-looking man at a gas pump in the middle of nowhere, fueling his black-60s-era muscle car. While making reference to the "responsibility" of a man at his age, the advertisement promotes a drug that "assists" and enhances sexual performance.[10] We aging men can "still have it," even if we need a little help.

I have thus shopped around for a better word than *maturity* to describe the aim of this book, but I have failed to find one. So I am going

9. We who work in academe easily fall prey to this temptation.

10. "Muscle car" is a term used for powerful, American-built sports cars of the (more or less) 1960s and '70s. The Chevy Camaro, the Pontiac GTO, and the Dodge Charger are examples of muscle cars. They exude a sense of sexual prowess and power.

to use it, hoping the reader will keep in mind that maturity in this case resembles that quality that developmental psychologist Erik Erikson had in mind with his term *generativity*. Both *maturity* and *generativity* refer to what can be considered as the most desired apex of life: when we've lived long enough to know what life is about and we have wisdom to share. Spiritual maturity thus points to that time when we are the most fruitful. It is a rich, glorious goal.

To get us headed in the right direction, therefore, let me introduce a Greek term found in the Bible. It is *telos*. A *telos* is a goal, and when the Bible uses this term, it means the same thing. It speaks to purpose and aim. To arrive at the goal is to fulfill the purpose for which God created and redeemed us. A related word is *teleios*, an adjective that is translated in English Bibles as "complete" or "mature" or even "perfect." The Bible makes clear that God's *telos* for believers is maturity—to become fully what God intends us to be. *Christian maturity therefore entails specific dispositions and behaviors that show the disciple becoming increasingly like Jesus for the sake of accomplishing Christ's purposes in the world.* For the sake of Christ's Kingdom, a mature disciple looks and acts like Jesus in the day-to-day messiness of real life.

This definition of Christian maturity is not new, and probably most readers would expect some idea of this sort, but it does raise certain unavoidable implications. First, having a grown-up faith requires that we think more systematically about discipleship, that we avoid lapsing into conventional but truncated ideas that give people the impression that they can adopt or focus on one "style" of Christian life and ignore another. I am thinking, for example, about how "discipleship" gets defined either as practices of inward piety (prayer, Bible reading, the other spiritual disciplines) or as acts of service (feeding the poor, clothing the naked, etc.). Mature Christians consistently integrate both—inward piety and outward ministry.

Secondly, the term *dispositions* reminds us of the need to pay proper attention to our emotional lives. We tend to treat feelings *sui generis*—of their own class—separate from thoughts and behaviors. This response produces unhappy results and, at the appropriate place, we will examine this problem in detail, but for now, I want to make clear that I do not mean that paying attention to our emotional lives calls for self-absorption. Our pop culture loves the drama of the reporter's "How did you feel when" question, asked of the victims of tragedy or the winners of championships. We talk much about our emotions, but we little understand them, particularly in relation to important theological concepts and especially with regard to their connection to our thoughts. Awareness of the interplay between thought and emotions in relation to Christian maturity therefore remains under-examined in our generation.[11]

Third, dispositions ultimately lead to actions. The word *disposition* itself means a characteristic tendency to act in a certain way in a given situation. Dispositions make evident the quality of our character. We are therefore talking about the fruit our lives produce. Sooner or later, the fruit becomes visible.

 For a moment, think of Christian maturity by way of someone who demonstrates the following qualities:

1. Growing biblical wisdom. Not only do they "know the Bible," they have so lived with the Bible's stories and teachings that they have a seasoned perspective that produces appropriate responses in real-life situations.

2. Genuine, consistent compassion expressed in such a way that others (believer and non-believer alike) are drawn to them for encouragement and help.

3. A demeanor of settled joy. This quality does not have anything to do with personality or situational happiness. Some people are loud and boisterous. Others are quiet and reserved. Joy is a persistent disposition that shines through a variety of personality types.

4. Care and gentle thoughtfulness in how they speak to other people, with words "seasoned with salt." It does not mean that they never say anything harsh or critical. It means that, even when they do have to speak the unvarnished truth, they consistently do so with deep concern for the wellbeing of the other in mind.

5. Long-term, sacrificial commitment in service to the common good of their Christian community and beyond. They are known for giving time, love, and material resources (whether meager or abundant) to others.

6. A transparent, teachable, humble openness toward others, a willingness to listen and learn from any quarter. If you know someone

11. This was not so with earlier generations of Christians, who actually had a robust vocabulary for discussing the emotional tone of their spiritual lives. For a fascinating discussion of this topic see Dixon, *From Passions to Emotions.*

who matches this description (and I desperately hope you do), then you know what Christian maturity looks like.

Being a grown-up Christian does not mean, of course, that we have no struggles. Quite to the contrary, a mature Christian lets people see their struggles, including their (to use an old term) "besetting sins." One qualification here: I am not suggesting that Christian maturity requires "hanging out dirty laundry" or sharing too much information. Transparency requires wisdom. Still, the humble, vulnerable transparency of a Christian who does not "have it all together" but who does demonstrate integrity and growth is powerful, indeed.

Now, think about how rare such Christians are by comparison to the vast number of professed Christians. Please remember: we are not merely talking about nice people engaging in lots of church activities. Our subject goes far beyond niceness. Mature Christians demonstrate courageous faith, doctrinal understanding, moral sensitivity, wisdom, and action that points people to Jesus and his Kingdom. Spiritually mature people look like Jesus. They are salt, light, and leaven, influencing people in redemptive ways.

One other important observation: grown-up Christians keep growing. Spiritual maturity is never a static state. It is always *a maturing maturity*. We have the blessed privilege of going from strength to strength as long as we live. As long as we live we can eagerly look forward to new levels of growth.

THE PLAN OF THIS BOOK

I have written this book to help people claim the vision of spiritual maturity as their own and to encourage us all to persevere toward it. To this end I will draw attention to a number of key orienting concerns and attempt to show not only their importance but also how they fit together and reinforce one another. In chapter 1, "The Goal of the Christian Life: Maturity," I offer a working definition and show that this vision is firmly embedded in the New Testament writings. A term like "spiritual maturity" is abstract, which makes it hard to identify. The New Testament will show us that the spiritually mature exhibit this quality in the context of specific situations. We will not find a comprehensive list, but we see the concreteness of spiritual maturity. God has set maturity as the goal for Christians. Chapter 1 helps us gain clarity about the goal.

In the second chapter, "The Focus of the Christian Life," we explore the Bible's use of the term *heart* in order to reclaim aspects of this term lost to awareness. We tend to reduce the notion of "heart" to enthusiasm or passion or sentiment. We commonly distinguish "heart" from "head," which is a big mistake. The Bible permits no such division. In order to redress this imbalance, this chapter will make use of recent scholarship in psychology and philosophy on the emotions to help interpret the Bible's teachings, and to cast a vision for what we can become.

I call chapter 3 "The Trajectory of Christian Maturity." Here we plot a number of recognizable periods and threshold moments in life so that, though people's experiences vary, we can follow a useful general pattern. The main purpose for this chapter is not merely to rehearse what may seem well known, but rather to suggest how people might find ways to identify where they are in their growth toward maturity. The trajectory also serves as a useful tool for leaders to analyze activities and programming in their ministries. The lion's share of congregational or small group programming seems to target the already committed, resulting in a smorgasbord approach to ministry. In this situation, leaders try to anticipate people's felt needs and offer specific experiences in order to capture as many participants as they can. People can use the trajectory to discern program effectiveness by assessing how people actually grow toward fulfilling God's Kingdom purposes.

The work on the trajectory of spiritual maturity prompts the question we will tackle in chapter 4. From where does the power come to change our hearts so that we actually *can* grow? Now that we have a better understanding of what the Bible means by "heart" and have a richer array of terms, what effects the change necessary for growth? Chapter 4 explores the popular, but inadequate, references to "grace" that drain the concept of the very power we need to realize the growth that we desire. Too often, we use "grace" either in doctrinal polemics (to figure out who is orthodox and who is heretical) or to avoid seeming too judgmental. Some people use the word to make sure everyone knows we do not believe in works righteousness, in other words, to declare that nothing we can do in our own strength merits salvation. Some use "grace" to mean a kind of indulgence, as in, "We should err on the side of grace," and since God is gracious, we get an endless supply of "do-overs," as if God were the source of infinite spiritual mulligans. To rebalance our understanding of grace, we will explore the concept as the action of God's Spirit to work in our hearts in sanctification and growth. Through the Spirit, God acts to heal and restore the image of God in us by imparting the qualities of Christ to us in body, mind, emotions, will, and practice.

My concerns about popular understandings and expressions of a term like grace point to another related challenge: our almost complete loss of vision for what sound doctrine actually does. Chapter 5 takes up perhaps the most difficult and contentious question of the book: what is the connection between good doctrine and a properly formed heart? We tend to think that doctrine functions primarily in relation to boundary matters or for intellectual purposes (logical consistency). People often use the idea of sound doctrine like a measuring stick or, worse, a shibboleth: "Does this person agree with us sufficiently to be a member of our group? Does that pastor (and church) preach sound doctrine?" What are we asking with such questions? It seems to me that we are asking, "Will I be spiritually *safe* if I join this group? Will I maintain my spiritual equilibrium and protect my destiny?" Attention to doctrine applies to a number of important topics, but in today's climate, it has very little to do with the formation of the heart.

As with the reduced understanding of "heart," our impoverished view of doctrine undercuts growth toward maturity. Since these topics can be contentious, I want to emphasize that I have no interest in setting up a false dichotomy between one recognized set of ideas versus another. In other words, I will not be asking people to dump wholesale their ideas about grace or their intellectual or polemical interest in doctrine and replace them with my "corrections." My concern has to do more with emphasis than picking just one position. Every generation tends to emphasize certain aspects of an idea or belief. I seek to expand and modify (thereby improving, to be sure) a current set of working notions by offering *additional* ideas to supplement and enrich spiritual life. I believe doing so will make the aim of spiritual maturity clearer and finding a path toward it more attainable.

Chapter 6 takes up the communal dimension of Christian maturity. It may seem odd to talk about a "mature group" (your congregation, your small group), but I will argue that what God does in individual human beings necessarily has a collective dimension as well. The Holy Spirit operates in the Body of Christ as a whole, as well as within individual believers' hearts. We dare not separate the individual from the communal, but too often we do. In fact, much of what American Protestants (at least) think about the Christian life is based on a hyper-individualized view, much to our detriment.

Appropriating the communal dimension of maturity into our thinking reminds us that we are deeply engaged in God's mission through the Holy Spirit working in our midst, not just in our individual lives. The Spirit guides us in contributing our part in fulfilling the commission Christ has given us for the world. Take a look at Eph 4:13, about growing into the full measure of the stature of Christ, then notice that the passage aims at the church as a whole and not merely individual believers. With this broader communal sense in mind, go back and scan the earlier chapters in Ephesians for how this collective witness embodies and witnesses to the power of God to transform the whole cosmos.

Finally, in chapter 7 we will focus on assessment. I admit that I have grown tired of the rampant pragmatism that tempts people always to go for what appears to be "practical." There is an endless supply of such books. You know them: how to share your faith (evangelism), how to pray, how to improve your financial situation by tithing, how to overcome depression, how to grow your marriage relationship or how to prepare for marriage or how to discipline children or how to defend the faith, get active in politics . . .

All these topics deserve serious attention, but the quick fix, five easy steps approach to the Christian faith is not getting the job of growing to maturity done, which is one of the main reasons that we seem unable even to recognize this goal and the call of God to press toward it. Everything in our culture screams that whatever "it" is that we're trying to do, we can find a shortcut to do it. As I have told my students numerous times, one of the key requirements of Christian discipleship is simply getting up and going to work every day as followers of Jesus. *There are simply no shortcuts to growth.*

AUTHOR'S ASSUMPTIONS

I appreciate writers who make their biases explicit and up front. It is now time, therefore, for me to state clearly my own, the guiding principles in this book. First, I desire to ground everything I advocate in Scripture. In other words, I assume scriptural authority. Saying that I believe in scriptural authority, however, is no shortcut for the hard work of interpretation. I will have to argue my case, rather than simplistically asserting what "the Bible says." I will work hard to show you the biblical, theological, and logical grounding for all my assertions.

Second, I stand in the Wesleyan tradition and will take a number of positions from that perspective, referring at several points to the teaching of John Wesley. When I invite you to spend time thinking about Wesley's explanation of Christian maturity, I am not asking you to become Wesleyan, if you are not already. I am asking you to think about key biblical themes and to use Wesley's guidance as a light to illumine your thinking, even if you prefer another Christian leader's conclusions.

I also draw on modern research in philosophy and psychology. I am fascinated, for instance, by the recent scholarly interest in a cognitive view of emotions—that emotions actually include cognitive content and can help us think clearly. For generations in Western thought, we have viewed the emotions mainly with suspicion—as upsetting good thinking. Recent explorations have produced more favorable points of view, with very interesting implications for how we think of and experience the Christian life.

Thus, my sources are (1) the Bible, understood at strategic points through (2) (mainly) the teachings of John Wesley, with (3) modern scholarship helping us see the contemporary relevance of the work. I hope, therefore, that by the time you have finished this book, you will feel confident that you have had adequate opportunity to examine my claims to see how they square with (and challenge) your own; you will have seen the sources I have used and how I used them, and you'll be able to judge whether I used them appropriately. Finally, you will have been able to decide if I argued my case well, whether my ideas flow logically from my assumptions and sources. In other words, you will have exercised your own power to discern the merits of this book. Most importantly, I pray that, by doing the methodological work, you will feel more confident and prepared to face challenges of spiritual growth on your way to maturity.

THE MISSION

Years ago, when my spouse, Joni, and I were living in Italy and I was a very young pastor of a fledgling expatriate congregation, I found myself during one particularly difficult period trying to figure out what being a pastor meant. I was strongly challenged by these words from Col 1:28–29, "It is he whom we proclaim, warning everyone and teaching everyone in all wisdom, so that we may present everyone *mature* in Christ [emphasis added]. For this I toil and struggle with all the energy that he powerfully inspires within me." As I continue in this journey, the sense of urgency in this vision—to help people understand biblical maturity and to pursue it energetically—only increases. For our sake, for the church's sake, for the Kingdom's sake, and for the world's sake, we Christians need to grow up.

1 The Goal
Spiritual Maturity

A heart in every thought renewed,
And full of love divine,
Perfect, and right, and pure, and good—
A copy, Lord, of thine![1]

A HARD TIME GROWING UP

Some years ago before I began working in higher education, I served as a pastor in small Kansas towns. In one place I served was a group of men about my age. We often ran around together doing guy things. We all shared an interest in college football, specifically of Kansas State University. Some of us were alumni and some just loved K-State. If you follow college football, you probably have heard of Coach Bill Snyder's turnaround of this program, taking it from one of the most hapless in college history to being a national contender. At the beginning of one season in this rise to glory, on a sunny Saturday afternoon, my friends and I headed for Manhattan (the "Little Apple") to watch the Wildcats play. We were wild with football fever.

We enjoyed the game (K-State won) and then, as alumni often do, we made a pass through Aggieville, for old times' sake. Aggieville is a small business district just off the southeast corner of the main campus. It is the local college student hangout and it was especially so back in our

---

1. Wesley, "O for a Heart to Praise My God." Emphasis added.

day (ah, the 1970s!). We decided to stop in Aggieville for a bite to eat and a bit of nostalgia before heading home.

We entered one of the establishments and sat down next to another table of men who looked to be about our age (at the time, pushing forty). They talked too loud. They flirted with the waitress—nearly half their age—by discussing various preferred sexual positions. They clearly had had too much to drink and generally made fools of themselves.

The thought hit me as I watched these men who were clearly of my generational cohort: "These guys are trying to relive their college days." It was as if they were trying to prove to themselves that, even though they were long out of college, they "still had it." A mixture of embarrassment and grief wafted over me.

I don't want to seem too much like a stick-in-the-mud or a killjoy. I firmly believe people should enjoy life. It is fun to reminisce about college days, because they are indeed a special time. But reminiscing by reverting to what most people regard as college boy silliness, behaviors that we should eventually leave behind, is entirely another matter. When grownups act like kids, it is embarrassing. No, it's worse than embarrassing. It is deeply troubling.

I could add other examples to this little scenario that strongly suggest that we Americans have an aversion to growing up. Because the oldest of the baby boom generation are entering retirement and because it is numerically so big, baby boom issues show up prominently in a variety of ways, from the movie *Wild Hogs*, to advertisements that play on our insecurities about getting old, to slogans like "Fifty is the new thirty." As sociologist Wade Clark Roof noted in his study of baby boomer spirituality, "While every generation undergoes a midlife passage of sorts, for boomers it is perhaps more traumatic. For a long time they knew only a youth culture—everybody around them, seemingly, was young, they were a persistently adolescent generation. 'We have dieted, jogged, and exercised so much,' comments boomer writer Lynn Smith, 'we look and actually *think* we are five to ten years younger than we are.'"[2]

We can celebrate the benefits of living more vigorously while growing old, but we should also notice the unhelpful aspects captured in this observation. I do not want to overdo my generalizations about the differing generations (baby boomers, Gen Xers, and now, the Millennials),

---

2. Roof, *A Generation of Seekers*, 248.

but it does appear that we are experiencing negative consequences across society. While desiring not to grow old too quickly, we also exhibit the penchant for not growing up. If the people who are supposed to be the grownups do not act like grownups, what impact does our immaturity have on younger generations?

This problem is particularly critical for followers of Jesus. In one sense we are facing an age-old challenge: how do Christians be *in* the world, but not *of* the world? More importantly, how do the values from popular culture—the passion to look and stay young and for self-expression and self-assertion—affect our understanding of the normal Christian life? Do we really want to experience the fullness of life as God intends, or do we want the vision of a full life that we create from the materials of pop culture? Immaturity shortchanges the blessing of life in Christ. But it also affects others. We who have been Christians for a while need to grow up for the sake of others, particularly the generations following us. Our growing to maturity in Christ is not just for our own sakes. It is for theirs. They need to see wisdom, stability, peacefulness, and loving, sacrificial service from us. We need to pass on the best of what we have learned in life. The world desperately needs grown-up Christians.[3]

SPIRITUAL MATURITY IS THE GOAL AND JESUS IS THE WAY

Let's start, then, with a working definition: a spiritually mature Christian is one whose whole character—*dispositions, words, and actions*—emulates the character of Jesus Christ himself. Each of these italicized words counts equally as the other two. Words and actions, of course, seem clear enough, but "dispositions" may need some definition. By "dispositions," I mean those tendencies to act in certain ways under certain circumstances. To be sure, we do not consciously think about such tendencies. They seem to "just happen," but, with reflection, we can see the combined thoughts, feelings, desires, and motives that lead to specific actions, hence the need to think about dispositions.

At the outset, then, we must resist the natural tendency to divide and reduce the concept of spiritual maturity into manageable parts. To show the importance of holding identifiable dimensions of spiritual growth

---

3. Remember the confusion people demonstrate about spiritual maturity, illustrated in the Barna Group survey mentioned in the introduction. The most common answer for a definition of spiritual maturity was "following the rules."

together, consider this example: You probably know someone who experienced a tragedy—the unexpected death of a loved one, for instance—who then stood on the receiving end of empty platitudes delivered matter-of-factly by an insensitive Christian. This Christian committed at least two mistakes all in one scenario: (1) in the rush to "comfort" did not sense the pathos of the moment for the sufferer, and (2) did not recognize the shallow inadequacy of the pious platitude. Think, now, about the word *disposition*. What prompted this no doubt well-meaning believer to act and to speak in such an insensitive, clueless way? The best answer to this question involves paying attention to the integration of a number of topics that we will cover in this book, topics having to do with how our thoughts and feelings work together.

In our time Christians have a reputation for simplistic beliefs, for insensitively mouthing empty platitudes, and for excluding "undesirable" people. I actually have a book on my shelf titled, *When Bad Christians Happen to Good People*. Honestly, I think this bad reputation gets overstated, yet we must face people's impressions even if we think they are not precisely accurate. Here we have one of those cases of perceptions being the reality we must face. What got us to this condition? Part of the problem is a simple loss of vision. We need to reclaim the goal of spiritual maturity as *our* goal.

Reclaiming this goal requires that we face squarely some challenging questions. First, is it realistic to think that we could not only aspire to look and act like our Lord but also in some recognizable way, achieve it? We know that the New Testament calls for us to grow in grace and faith. Second Peter 3:18 makes this point explicitly: "But grow in the grace and knowledge of our Lord and Savior Jesus Christ." Likewise, Eph 4:15 says, "But grow up in every way into him who is the head, into Christ." Still, what does this mean?

To answer this question requires our taking some time to delve into profound theological ideas having to do with the nature of Christ. The technical term theologians use for this work is *Christology*, the study of the nature and work of Jesus the Christ. If we his followers are to give evidence of his character in our lives, we need to consider what his nature is like, which immediately poses a problem. How can we be like Jesus if Jesus is divine? It is relatively easy for us to grasp what Jesus has done for us in dying on the cross and rising from the dead. We can love Jesus for what he has done, but how do we sinful humans emulate a holy God?

To answer this question requires that we look at the other side of Jesus' nature—his human nature. This calls for exploring another central claim: the Incarnation (becoming human) of the Son of God. For help in this regard, I turn to the work of an early church leader, Irenaeus, bishop of Lyons (ca. 130–200). Christian tradition links him to the apostolic age through Bishop Polycarp back to the Apostle John. As bishop, Irenaeus was charged with strengthening the faithful and defending against heretics. He wrote a work, *Against Heresies*, in which he took up this question of the Incarnation and argued against claims about Jesus' nature that radically altered the basic understanding of Christian faith. This deeply theological disagreement bears directly upon Christian life, not just thought. In the summary that follows, pay close attention to terms, and then we will consider how these ideas would have had a huge impact on how people actually experience the Christian faith.

Irenaeus sought to refute two competing and somewhat contrasting claims about Jesus, both of which ran counter to the developing tradition of christological thought within the church. Some heretics claimed that "Jesus" and "the Son" were actually two distinct and separable beings. In this view "the Son" (who *is* divine[4]) *came upon* the human Jesus, but the two natures—divine and human—remained separate. Accordingly, Jesus the man remained merely human while being "inhabited" for a time by the (divine) Son. Another group claimed, on the other hand, that Jesus had only one divine nature. In other words, he only *appeared*[5] to be human.

Now we can start to see how these ideas would dramatically change the understanding of Jesus' work. In the first case, if this claim is true, then Jesus died the death of an ordinary human being. The divine nature—which couldn't die—departed from Jesus immediately before his death. In the second case, if Jesus only appeared to be human, then he only appeared to die, since deity cannot die. In the first case, we would have to ask, "What does the death of an ordinary human being accomplish? Does it support the fundamental claim that Jesus died for our sins? How could an ordinary human being's death accomplish a feat of such

---

4. We're in some pretty deep theological water here. In using the word *divine*, I encourage the reader not to think of God in the usual, Christian sense. The heretics were importing ideas of divinity from other philosophical and mythical sources that cannot be examined here.

5. This heresy is known as Docetism, from the Greek word *dokeo*, which means "to seem" or "to appear."

magnitude?" In the second case, if Jesus did not actually die, then the whole claim about his death for the world's salvation is false.

Do you see how each claim radically alters our basic understanding of the significance of Jesus, which would change our understanding of the Christian faith? These concerns motivated Bishop Irenaeus to write that "Jesus" and "the Son" were not separate beings, but that Jesus was *both* truly God *and* truly human: "[The heretics] thus wander from the truth, because their doctrine departs from Him . . . who is always present with the human race, *united to and mingled with His own creation . . . and who became flesh . . . who did also suffer for us,* [emphasis added] and rose again on our behalf, and who will come again in the glory of His Father, *to raise up all flesh* [emphasis added]."[6] A couple of sentences later, Irenaeus adds, "And thus He took up [human nature] into himself."[7]

This "taking up" of human nature by the Son of God has tremendous implications for Christian discipleship. We can see that Jesus' death on the cross as the Perfect Substitute, the Lamb of God, effects forgiveness and change of status for us. We move from guilty sinners to forgiven saints. This is God doing something *for* us. But that the Son of God assumed our nature also points to the impact of salvation in terms of the actual transformation of our natures and the possibility of full restoration of God's image in us. The Incarnate Word of God became human in order to change the way we are! This is God doing something *in* us. The becoming human of the Word of God is the first step in transforming human nature.

Now, think about what this teaching says about God. God could have healed and saved humans any way he chose. God chose to enter into human nature (see Phil 2:5–11) and redeem it by fully sharing our life. That God would so identify with us is amazing beyond words. What kind of God would do such a thing? A God of holy, omnipotent love.[8] In love, God-the-Word took human flesh and lived the full human experience, from conception to death. This claim *makes his entire life important for Christian discipleship*, not just his death and resurrection. Salvation, from this angle, includes not just being freed from the penalty of sin, but also being delivered from its power, so that we can live like Jesus. Hopefully, in

6. Irenaeus, *Against Heresies*, 1:442. Emphasis added.

7. Ibid., 1:443.

8. A current argument among scholars is how to understand the traditional doctrine of God's omnipotence. I am here upholding that doctrine—God's power is limited only by God's own holy nature and nothing else.

this brief description of a theological debate, we can see how ideas shape how we experience Christian life.

At a later point in the book, in the chapter on grace, we will explore more fully how the power for living a life that emulates Christ is applied to his disciples. We will take another step in looking at what God is doing *in* us, by the power of the Holy Spirit. For now, we are concentrating on the point that Jesus Christ is the Model and Exemplar of the Christian life. If we want to see how to live the Christian life, we are to look at Jesus.

Certain Scriptures, read with Irenaeus's guidance, therefore, start to gather more force, relative to Jesus as Exemplar and Model. In Rom 5:12–21, for example, we see Paul drawing a somewhat unbalanced parallel between Adam and Christ. Adam is a "type" of the "one who was to come," (Rom 5:14). And as death came into the world through one man (Adam), justification for sin came into the world through the grace of one man, Jesus Christ (5:15). This teaching from Paul suggests a deep connection in God's design between Adam (as representing all humanity) and Christ (as also representing all redeemed humanity). Even though, in this Romans passage, Paul has focused on Christ's death, his linking Adam and Christ challenges us to grapple with the full scope of Jesus' life as the Last Adam. As well as being the divine Son, in Jesus' death we see the Perfect Human offering his life in substitute for our own. When we look at Jesus' life, then, we can see God's design for us humans.

Similarly, in 1 Cor 15:45, Paul writes, "Thus it is written, 'The first man Adam became a living being'; the last Adam became a life-giving spirit." Again we see reference to the humanity of Jesus (the Last Adam) as having a saving impact. In both Scriptures, Paul connects Jesus' atoning work not just to his divinity, but also to his humanity. Without intending to weaken the significance of Jesus' death on the cross as central to our salvation, I am suggesting that this 1 Corinthians text points also to the belief that the way Jesus lived has saving effect.

Likewise, in Heb 12:2, we read the call to look to Jesus, the Pioneer and Perfecter of our faith. Another version says that he is Author and Finisher. Differing translations can suggest one emphasis over another, but with Pioneer and Perfecter, we get the impression of Jesus as the One who goes ahead of us on the path that we follow. And we are to consider his life an example as we follow that same path.[9] If, then, Jesus is fully

9. Again, for any reader who may be well aware of some of the Christological controversies, I worry that my comments here imply that I am questioning Jesus' full divinity. I

human as well as fully divine, we can take his life *as exemplary for us.* Not only did Jesus die our death on the cross, but he has also lived our life. His living it shows us the way to live. By the power of his Spirit working within us, we are enabled to live like him.

THE NEW TESTAMENT AND SPIRITUAL MATURITY[10]

Keeping this theological background in mind, we return to our definition of spiritual maturity: a spiritually mature believer demonstrates the dispositions, words, and actions of Jesus himself. Hopefully, after the foregoing description of the significance of Jesus' whole life, we can see how he sets the standard. To grow to maturity, therefore, demands our whole selves, our complete love and allegiance to Jesus as Lord and to all that he stands for. Therefore, every part of life comes under our Lord's scrutiny and direction. While we admit that we often fall short of the aim, we can never settle for anything less than the goal of full-grown spiritual adulthood.

Let us begin to piece together some concrete ideas about what spiritual maturity looks like in real life by turning to the New Testament passages that explicitly refer to maturity as the goal. With each reference we will see maturity with respect to some particular situation or concern and in each case it involves combined (integrated) thoughts, feelings, words, and actions. In the Scriptures, maturity is never merely an abstract ideal to which we nod then conveniently forget. By the time we finish the survey, we will have a reasonably clear picture that spiritual maturity truly is the goal, and that goal is for us to look like Jesus.

In the Greek New Testament, virtually every time we see the terms "mature," "perfect," or "complete," it translates the word *teleios*, a derivative of *telos*, which means "goal" or "aim" or "end." If *telos* is the goal, then *teleios* means arriving at or accomplishing the goal. In the Christian life, we aim at the goal of fully embodying the nature and purposes of God revealed in Christ. We have been redeemed for this very aim.

One important caveat regarding terminology: we tend to think of "perfect" as "flawless." The Bible does not mean "flawless" when it uses

am not. But notice how awareness of the controversies and a person's conclusions about them affects the reading of my words now.

10. Remember, I am following the New Revised Standard Version translation. If you use another version, you will find "mature," "perfect," and "complete" used interchangeably.

teleios, even when translated into English as "perfect." Biblical "perfect" does not require "flawless." We will run into "perfect" several times, so it will be important to remind ourselves of what the word does *not* mean as well as what it means. With this caution in mind, we start at the beginning of the New Testament and work toward the end.

In the Sermon on the Mount, Jesus says, "Be perfect, therefore, as your heavenly Father is perfect" (Matt 5:48). Wait a minute! Must we start this way? Obviously, no one can be perfect like the Father, so what did Jesus mean? This difficult verse reminds us of the importance of reading Bible statements in their context, which, in this case, helps us understand the specific situation to which "perfect" refers.

Jesus' injunction to be perfect comes as the conclusion to a unit that starts with 5:21, "You have heard that it was said to those of ancient times, 'You shall not murder.'"[11] In this section we find injunctions about anger, adultery, divorce, swearing oaths, retaliation, and love for enemies. The concept, "perfect," therefore, ties to these particular teachings about specific kinds of relationships: don't demean people with angry, cruel words, practice faithfulness in marriage that extends even to our thoughts, and love enemies and pray for them. We show maturity in Christ (and prove our relationship to the Father) by exemplifying these particular attitudes and actions. If we want to get a feel for whether we are growing toward maturity, then, we'll have to ask how we're doing with Jesus' call on these particular questions.

How are you doing, for example, on the "loving your enemies" question? The concept is easy enough to grasp, but the actual doing is another matter. What does it mean to love one's enemy? Can I even identify my enemies? Can I *love* my enemy yet not *like* her/him? (You've probably heard this dodgy distinction.) Certainly, we can *act* in loving and peaceable ways and, in that sense, love our enemies, without *feeling* particularly warm or affectionate toward them. However, I do not think this rationale matches Jesus' teaching. (Remember Paul's words in Rom 5:10; at one time all of us were enemies of Christ.) If we want to be mature, when we love our enemies, we *feel something* for them. I can't really love someone in a mature way and feel cold and distant from that person all the time.

Thus, spiritual maturity has something quite direct and challenging to say about the nature of our relationships. We can start to practice

11. See Betz, *Sermon on the Mount*, 321.

aiming at the goal of maturity by asking ourselves these deeply important questions. How are we doing in our relationships? How do we speak about our opponents? What attitude do we demonstrate toward those people who do not share our religious beliefs? And since we are just beginning to practice, let's remember not to reduce spiritual maturity to mere action. It will not do to manage, for example, to speak kind-sounding words to an enemy while we harbor hate in our hearts. To grow spiritually, we must also deal with the reality of the hate in our hearts as well as practice speaking kindly to enemies.

The next reference to maturity comes in relation to wealth in Matt 19:21. Jesus told the rich young man, "If you wish to be perfect, go, sell your possessions, and give the money to the poor . . . then come, follow me." Almost nothing makes us more nervous than when people start talking about money. It is very easy to distract ourselves with debates about whether one economic system is closer to the Christian faith than another, but this misses the point. Though the rich young man was righteous in many ways, his withholding his wealth and possessions barred him from the fullness of life Jesus offered. (To be mature, we cannot withhold anything from Christ's lordship.) Thus, the spiritually mature recognize in attitude and action that following Jesus takes precedence over making sure they live at a certain material standard.

Let's see if we can practice holding our own feet to the fire regarding wealth. I assume that most people reading this book live at a reasonably comfortable middle-class standard. Likewise, most of us reading this book will continue to live at the financial level we're living at now. The temptation is always to turn this conversation between the rich young man and Jesus into some kind of morality tale, with the result that we distort "the moral" into an abstract rule that disconnects it from having actually to follow Jesus. Even talking about "generosity" (notice the abstraction?) does not touch what this story dramatizes. *Living responsively to Jesus' call for all our possessions* does. To grow spiritually, we practice avoiding the abstract, rule-driven approach to wealth and practice laying all that we own at Jesus' feet. We still possess things, but differently, knowing that—to follow Jesus—we may be called upon to give up something specific and precious for the sake of his work. This is a most difficult thing to do, since wealth has power. That is why we're talking about maturity—about a grown-up faith.

Recently, I got a glimpse of this matter. My wife and I attended two fundraising dinners on two successive days, one related to the university where I work and the other for a local urban ministry. Each dinner had the same number of tables, with roughly the same number of people attending. The first involved very wealthy and some well-known people. As university chaplain, I was called upon to offer the invocation. We sat with people who financially support this particular endeavor. They knew why they'd been invited and are generous supporters.

The very next day we attended a luncheon to raise money for an inner-city ministry. At this venue the stars of the show were a group of school-aged Latino children, most of them from families living in difficult to desperate conditions. The children had collected 16,400 *pennies* (!) to buy nets for children in Africa to protect them from malaria-carrying mosquitoes.

I love God's math. At each dinner, we met conscientious, compassionate people. Some of them have incredible resources, which they share generously. Others have little, but still share with compassion and staggering generosity. I will long remember these two days, and I think it helps me understand something about what Jesus was saying to that wealthy young man. Ultimately, it does not matter how much or how little we have. What matters is whether we recognize that it all belongs to Jesus.

We find the next reference to maturity in 1 Cor 2:6, "Yet among the mature we do speak wisdom, though it is not a wisdom of this age." Here Paul makes a distinction in kinds of wisdom to shed light on the problem of schism in the Corinthian church. Some identified who were "truly wise" by measuring them according to the standard-bearers of wisdom in their day, but they had two different concepts of wisdom at their disposal, both of them dangerous from a Christian point of view.[12] Thus, Paul wanted the Corinthians to avoid, first, the speculative, abstract "wisdom" that deludes people into thinking that by possessing this "wisdom" they are more valuable than other people. The second kind of "wisdom" involved the mystery cults into which applicants had to be initiated, which similarly gave them a false sense of superior status relative to the uninitiated. One kind of wisdom points to an intellectual problem while the other kind points to a religious one. The arrogance of superiority in each case belies the wisdom.

---

12. See Fitzmyer, *First Corinthians*, 174.

In contrast, the spiritually mature, Paul says, are "foolish" enough to trust a God who appears weak, but who conquers sin in that "weakness" and "foolishness." The mature refuse to let anything separate them into status groups or hold themselves aloof from "lesser" believers. Such wisdom shows moral courage. (Remember how difficult it is to stand up to people who have any kind of worldly power, whether intellectual, economic, or social.) The wisdom of Christ that looks foolish to the world is made visible by the spiritually mature. Their humility contributes to the unity and strength of the Body of Christ.[13]

Next, consider 1 Cor 14:20, "Brothers and sisters, do not be children in your thinking; rather, be infants in evil, but in thinking be adults."[14] "Adults" in this verse translates the Greek plural *teleioi* (mature, complete, perfect ones), the same term we have been tracking. The context here points to two specific concerns: (1) order and decency in worship and (2) whom we should keep in mind when having our arguments about worship. The specific issue has to do with speaking in tongues. Those with this gift evidently had gotten the idea that they were somehow spiritually superior to those who did not have it. An elitist attitude—like the problem with "the wise" that we just discussed—had begun to creep into and divide the community. Imagine being a visitor and entering worship in which the community was this badly divided (maybe it's not so hard to imagine). You could feel the tension as people spoke in tongues without interpretation, prompting others to get angry.[15]

"Being adult in thinking," therefore, suggests practicing a watchful attitude in which people understand two important principles. First, remember the purpose of worship. Second, remember who might be adversely affected when believers exhibit unchristian attitudes when they disagree. Certainly, we need to speak our minds and openly address differences of opinion, but we do so in view of the conviction that we belong to each other in Christ and to avoid wounding the spiritually fragile.

13. There are serious implications in this point for those of us who teach others, who might enjoy too much the status we gain from being teachers.

14. Fitzmyer, *First Corinthians*, suggests that the exhortation to be "adult" in thinking alludes to Paul's comment in chapter 13, about moving from childhood ("When I was a child . . .") to adulthood ("But when I became a man, I put away childish things . . ."), which fits well with the trajectory toward adulthood that we are tracing in this book.

15. If this seems far-fetched, remember that this same congregation had members who got drunk at the Lord's Table. See 1 Cor 11:17–22.

Spiritual maturity requires, then, that we learn to hold our tongues in some cases, speak gently (even if straightforwardly) in others, and always love and esteem brothers and sisters in the Body, even when we disagree. Remember, the world is watching.

Again, let's pause to practice thinking about what aiming at spiritual maturity would entail, were we to take seriously this passage from 1 Corinthians. Again, we cannot simplistically focus on behavior. When we're in the middle of a church disagreement and our emotions run high, if we have not practiced and honed our dispositions, then we will speak and act in ways not befitting the Gospel. To grow spiritually, we need to practice forethought, humbly learning to recognize our tendencies and prayerfully practicing to gain new dispositions.

Our next reference to maturity comes in Eph 4:13, and it is particularly important: "Until we all come to the unity of the faith and of the knowledge of the Son of God, to maturity, to the *measure of the full stature of Christ* . . ." [emphasis added]. The New Revised Standard Version takes some liberty here by translating the Greek into "to maturity" rather than the more literal *eis andra teleion*, "to a mature man." Paul[16] is speaking to the whole church, not just to individual Christians. To make clear that Paul is referring to a quality of maturity prescribed for *all* in the church, the New Revised Standard Version uses the abstract noun "maturity," thus drawing attention to the fact that *no one in the church is exempt* from the call to maturity. The standard for maturity is Christ himself: "the measure of the full stature of Christ."

Again, as we have done with the preceding Scriptures, we look to the context to understand maturity with respect to a specific life concern. In this passage we discover that spiritual maturity has to do with building up the Body of Christ *for the sake of Christ's ministry in the world*. Growing to maturity thus keeps us properly aimed at this mission. Christ has given the church gifts so that it can engage in his mission. Therefore, we speak the truth in love, and we encourage and build up the community *in order that* we can all serve as Christ intends.

Here we find a very important point about spiritual maturity: it matters to the church that you exercise your gift. We don't grow to maturity apart from one another and without each other. And it's crucial that we understand the logic of the Body of Christ. "You" and "I" absolutely

16. I am aware of the scholarly disagreement over the authorship of Ephesians. I use Paul as author for simplicity's sake.

need each other to grow to maturity. And the world needs "us" to grow to maturity. Our growing to maturity is crucial for doing the work that Christ's Body is supposed to do. Spiritual maturity thus means long-term commitment to exercise our gifts according to Christ's "gifting" us, for the sake of Christ's work in the world. The counterfactual is also true: if you do not exercise your spiritual gift for ministry, you do not grow spiritually.

Next we come to Phil 3:14–15: "I press on toward the goal for the prize of the heavenly call of God in Christ Jesus. Let those of us then who are *mature* [complete, perfect] be of the same mind." Notice the action of pressing on. It suggests persistent and sustained effort. Growing to maturity is not easy. It takes effort, focus, discipline, self-awareness, humility, and honesty. Second, those who are mature are to "be of the same mind." "Be of the same mind" translates the Greek imperative verb *phroneite*. "Mind" means more than mental activity, more than mere logic. It includes a certain attitude that people growing to maturity share for each other. It hearkens back to Phil 2:5: "Have this mind in you which was also in Christ Jesus." In fact, the same imperative verb form—*phroneite*—appears in both places. The *Theological Dictionary of the New Testament* says, "*Phroneite* connotes *will* and *disposition* as well as the usual cognitive functions."[17] This word thus draws on the whole content of our hearts: our desires, dreams, values, and yearnings, which lead to actions to fulfill those goals. Again, as we saw with Eph 4:13, we see here that spiritual maturity involves what we share, *what we are* as a community. All Christians, according to the example Paul himself sets, are to "press on toward the goal" and some in the Philippian community are demonstrating that degree of maturity, such that Paul could address them specifically.

Moving on to Col 1:28–29: "It is [Christ] whom we proclaim, warning everyone and teaching everyone in all wisdom, so that we may present everyone mature [complete, perfect] in Christ." The same word, *teleios*, that we have tracked elsewhere, appears here, too. With this verse we can add the role of doctrine to the description of spiritual maturity. Whereas having a head full of orthodox ideas does not automatically translate to growth, it also does not mean that we can safely ignore doctrine. In fact, it is impossible to have *no* doctrine.

17. Kittel, *Theological Dictionary of the New Testament*, 9:233. Emphasis added.

We encounter here the problem of a common caricature of doctrine. For those who worry about its divisive effects, "doctrine" usually means abstract, disembodied concepts—coupled with arguments about which ideas are orthodox (correct) and which are heretical—that seem to have literally nothing to do with how we actually live. We live in a pragmatist society, which values above all those teachings that seem to "work." This practical quality makes such teachings seem "relevant." Conversely, we can therefore stop worrying about ideas that seemingly have no practical relevance. In a later chapter I will demonstrate the formative power of doctrine on our hearts, showing that doctrine goes far beyond academic concepts. Clearly, Paul is not concerned in Colossians 1 with academic abstractions. If we want to grow toward maturity, we will grapple with ideas about the Christian faith that shape our hearts and make a difference in the way we live and serve in the world.

We find a similar concern for doctrine in the book of Hebrews, in which forms of *teleios* appear explicitly in four places. The first two mark the beginning and end of a unit. Hebrews 5:14 states, "But solid food is for the mature, for those whose faculties have been trained by practice to distinguish good from evil." At the end of this unit stands Heb 6:1, "Therefore, let us go on toward perfection, leaving behind the basic teaching about Christ, and not laying again the foundation: repentance from dead works and faith toward God." Both the relevant terms "mature" and "perfection" translate a form of the same Greek word we have been following throughout this study. Notice the sense of movement that "going on to" suggests. "Perfection/maturity" is a state, but not a steady state.

As usual, we are breaking into the middle of an extended argument, which, in this case, has to do with a particular expression of immaturity that the book of Hebrews addresses. The immature seem to keep going over and over questions on some of the basic doctrines of the faith: "repentance from dead works and faith toward God, instruction about baptism," and so on. This going-over is not for lack of conceptual clarity. It does not have in mind those who might say, "I don't yet understand," as in "I do not yet grasp the meaning." Rather, it has to do with believing—with whether or not to place one's full weight of trust on those basic teachings. In light of this concern, then, the whole structure of the book of Hebrews addresses this temptation to neglect or even leave the Christian faith. It does so by pointing to the superiority of Christ with regard to a number of traditional beliefs and practices that apparently tempt some within the Hebrews community to give up on what they have learned of Christ:

- He is superior to the angels (God's messengers), chapter 1.
- He is superior to Moses, chapter 3.
- He is the superior High Priest, chapters 4–5.
- He is the Mediator of a better covenant, chapter 8.
- His sacrifice for sin is superior to animal sacrifice and renders such sacrifice useless and meaningless, chapters 9–10.

So, what is the problem regarding maturity or lack thereof? Waning confidence in Christ. Despite the fact that the Lord had revealed himself to earlier witnesses and had demonstrated that same presence among contemporary leaders, some of the folks are struggling to hold steady in faith. Enough time has passed between the original events of the Gospel and the writing of Hebrews that some people have started wondering if the Story is really believable. Chapter 2 begins with an exhortation: "Therefore we must pay greater attention to what we have heard so that we may not drift away from it" (Heb 2:1).

Consider how Hebrews helps us think about spiritual maturity: the spiritually mature recognize the worthlessness of endlessly interrogating the Gospel Story in order to dispel all doubt and provide unassailable certainty. Constantly shifting back and forth between two half-positions bespeaks the double-mindedness criticized in the book of James. In truth, it reveals disbelief. There is nothing particularly "intellectual" about suspending belief in a state of perpetual agnosticism. Doing so bespeaks fear, not intellectual virtue. The constant rehashing of basic points thwarts one's growth rather than enhancing it.

Perhaps my summary still seems opaque, so let me try an analogy. A while back, my wife and I enjoyed a trip to the Pacific Ocean side of Mexico. One day as we were lounging on the beach, I noticed an elderly couple at the water's edge. It was a windy day and the waves were somewhat high, but not especially threatening. The husband had his arm around his wife and gently coaxed her closer and closer to the waves. She hesitantly inched forward, but, as the waves began to break, she scurried back to a safer, drier place on the beach. Several times the couple repeated this dance. On that day, I never saw the woman actually enter the surf. It was clear that she wanted to do so, but could not bring herself to do it.

As I read the warnings in the book of Hebrews, I get a similar impression. Unlike the woman on the beach, the people to whom Hebrews was written actually had entered the water, so to speak. They had "tasted the heavenly gift and have shared in the Holy Spirit" (Hebr 6:4), but for a variety of reasons—neglect, doubt—the temptation to repudiate their faith in Christ loomed always near. Notice the outcome. An attitude (fear or discouragement) prompts an action, which, in turn (for the Hebrews) thwarts growth.[18]

The last reference to maturity that we will consider comes from Jas 1:4: "And let endurance have its full effect, so that you may be mature and complete, lacking in nothing." "Full effect" translates *teleion,* and "mature," *teleioi* (plural). In the Christian life, endurance may be among the most difficult of character qualities to assimilate and practice. Though we live by God's grace, effort and struggle attend spiritual growth. I realize I state the obvious, but how often do Christians give up in discouragement before reaching their envisioned goal? "It's not working." "It's too difficult." "I'm not getting anything out of it." James clearly makes the connection between sustained effort and the soundness of our spiritual lives. If we give up on the struggle toward maturity, we preempt even the possibility of growing to maturity.

It seems fitting that the theme of perseverance from the book of James provides the stopping place for our survey of New Testament verses on spiritual maturity. As the book of Revelation also notes, the situation in which we find ourselves today calls for endurance: "Here is a call for the endurance of the saints, those who keep the commandments of God and hold fast to the faith of Jesus" (14:12). Endurance requires focus and courage. Growing to maturity is not easy and, sadly, we twenty-first-century Western Christians seem too often to want things easy. Until we dispel this notion from our list of desires, however, growth toward maturity will be impossible. But it is demanded of those who follow Jesus.

We have come to the end of our look at references to spiritual maturity in the New Testament. At the minimum, this study shows that the vision of maturity cannot remain a minor side issue in the Christian life. It

18. This point receives emphasis in Heb 10:1, in which the temptation to return to some form of following the Law is lifted up as fundamentally counterproductive: "Since the law has only a shadow of the good things to come and not the true form of these realities, it can never, by the same sacrifices that are continually offered year after year, make perfect those who approach."

actually feels quite odd to write these words, since no one seriously questions the belief that Christians are supposed to grow spiritually. Yet, in the hectic pace of modern life, we seem largely to have lost sight of the goal.

NOT JUST THESE PASSAGES

In this chapter, I have stuck with passages that explicitly use words like "mature" or "perfect" or "complete," but the Bible has plenty to say in more than just these places. Consider Gal 5:22–23, for example, with the description of the fruit of the Spirit. If a Christian were to demonstrate these qualities, would that person not show the attitudes and actions of Christ himself? There is a parallel, then, between the fruit of the Spirit and the character of Jesus. If we could consistently embody such qualities, would we not truly be mature Christians?

Furthermore, notice the emotion-tone of the fruit: love, joy, peace, patience and so on. You cannot consistently act kind and gentle without *being* kind and gentle, which means *showing the disposition of* compassion and love for people. (If Jesus felt compassion, then, to be like him, we feel similar compassion.) You cannot express joy without feeling joy. When we ignore or drain all the emotion out of a text like Gal 5:22–23, we wind up with all sweat and work, no joy. But as the songwriter Michael Card has reminded people for a long time, "There is a joy in the journey. There is a light in the love on the way . . . and freedom for those who obey."[19]

This survey gives us reference points to put some flesh on the skeleton concept of spiritual maturity. We show spiritual maturity always in connection to specific situations, through which we demonstrate the very character of Christ himself. Like Jesus, we love our enemies. We hold possessions loosely, remembering that they really do belong to the Lord. We strive for quality relationships within the Body of Christ. We work hard for peace in the community, not by avoiding conflict and blurring differences, but by speaking with love and humility, knowing that the spiritual health of seekers is damaged by petty squabbles. We pay attention to sound doctrine until the Spirit gives birth to faith in our hearts and we confidently, consistently move forward, rather than getting suspended in semi-faith. Finally, we accept that maturity is a lifelong journey and we persevere in it.

19. Card, "Joy in the Journey."

The work we have done in this chapter sets the bar high. Let us encourage ourselves with two critical observations:

1. The Christian life is not a treadmill—a lot of effort while staying in the same place. It is a journey made with friends—our Friend, Elder Brother and Chief Shepherd—as well as our friends on earth.

2. God is invested in and committed to our maturity. God's grace (the Holy Spirit's action) is sufficient for all our weaknesses. Growing to maturity requires effort, but it does not require that we feel strong and capable. Christ's strength is made perfect in our weakness.

Now that we have some idea of what spiritual maturity looks like, we can take the next step and consider the seat and center of maturity. The term we use—"heart"—is deceptively familiar, but let us not go to sleep. We have some serious work to do.

2 The Focus of the Christian Life
The Heart

> I began to see that true religion was seated in the heart, and that God's law extended to all our thoughts as well as words and actions.
>
> —John Wesley

In the neighborhood through which I drive to work, the traffic lights near a school zone have timer displays on the pedestrian crossing signs. After a few seconds to let pedestrians pass, the display starts to blink a countdown, "10-9-8-7 . . ." Just as it hits "0," the traffic light changes to yellow.

On those days when I've cut myself a bit short on time and have a full appointment schedule awaiting me at the office, this timer display becomes the enemy. I'm driving to work, head full of the day's busy schedule, and I spy the countdown, knowing what it means: "4-3-2 . . ." I begin to gauge distance and speed. If I calculate that I'll make the light easily, I relax. If not, I feel the anxiety rise and I begin to fret.

This technological wonder has become a prompt for reflection on a core function of spiritual life, on the integrated mental actions that we usually call "thought," but which involves much more than mere mental processing. In this drive-time scenario we notice *three* sets of integrated mental operations. First is straightforward cognition. Through my visual sense, I notice relevant features of the external environment and begin assessing the situation. But while doing this mental calculation (cognition, thinking), I also feel mounting anxiety (emotion). I begin to think of how having to wait on the light would upset my finely balanced appointment schedule. I begin to berate myself (adding to the frustration) for not allowing more time to get to work. I worry about successfully making it through the light so that I can keep that appointment. Notice how the feelings of anxiety and the thoughts correlate.

A third operation goes in tandem with the others. Given the variables of the situation, I must decide on the best plan of action. We call this choosing an act of the will, but it turns out that the will is not just about choice. It also has to do with desire, attitude, and disposition. (Notice the emotional tonality of these words.) As I near the intersection and begin to realize that I will not easily make the light, I start to grapple with conflicting desires. Just how "pink" am I willing to let the light become before I feel that I'm unacceptably breaking the law? Do I wait for the light or charge through the intersection? What "moves" my will in this moment?

The Bible refers to this *integrated wholeness* of identifiable mental operations as "the heart," a term we find *nearly a thousand times* in the Scriptures. It demonstrates the centrality of this concept for a proper biblical understanding of human nature. The power of the heart's inclinations can frighten or confuse us. Well might we cry out, like the prophet Jeremiah, "The heart is devious above all else; it is perverse—who can know it?" (Jer 17:9). But we also know that our hearts have great capacity for love and, most importantly, for loving God. As Saint Augustine wrote at the beginning of his *Confessions*, "You have made us for yourself, and our heart is restless till it rests in you."[1]

The biblical concept of the heart has not fared well in the modern (or, if you prefer, postmodern) world. We regularly separate head and heart, for example, in ways that the Bible does not. For a variety of reasons that we do not have time to summarize but whose impact we need to acknowledge, we have learned to chop up human nature into discrete functions to the detriment of our spiritual growth. One of the most common manifestations of this problem within the church is a phenomenon I'll call the two-step.

---

1. Augustine, *Confessions*, 43.

THE PROBLEM OF THE TWO-STEP

American society deeply values knowledge and skills. I have been working in higher education for a while now, and we regularly talk about what makes for an excellent college education. Almost always, the talk turns to the twin concerns of knowledge and skills, that is, what students need to know and what they need to be able to do. "Majors"—coursework in a particular area[2]—structure students' academic lives *in order to* position them for a good job or go to graduate school. Everybody has to have a major. A college education is designed with unwavering focus on knowledge and skill with regard to these majors. The right kind of knowledge and skill leads to the kind of career that one wants. Knowledge and skill lead to success, right?

Not necessarily. It depends on what we include in terms like "knowledge" and "skill." Researchers have started noticing that mere intellectual ability (IQ) and the skill to "get things done" do not by themselves make good, effective leaders or workers. It also takes—to use the title of a book by Daniel Goleman—emotional intelligence.[3] If, for example, we do not exercise compassion and empathy, no matter how intelligent or technologically skillful we may be, we will be "dumb" in real life, undermining the very desires we have for success and fruitfulness.

We find a similar tendency in Christian teaching. I call it the two-step, but it has nothing to do with dancing. Step 1: we strive to "understand." To understand means to mentally grasp an idea, to "get it." If we can cognitively grasp a concept, we say that we "know it." Then comes step 2: we put the idea to work; we "apply." To apply means that we attempt to take action. We work on making some sort of change in attitude and practice.

Notice the assumptions. If we understand a principle, then we can put it to work. If we can put it to work, we will grow. But, in fact, we don't always grow because we don't always put it to work. Or, if we do, we do not always persevere. And sometimes even if we persevere, we do not realize the envisioned outcome. In fact, I think that many sincere Christians are frustrated by all the effort that seems to produce so little difference in

2. Sometimes they have more than one major, or a minor field of study. Almost always, they undertake these heavy loads in order to make themselves more marketable in the workplace. The knowledge/skill assumption is dominant.

3. Goleman, *Emotional Intelligence*. See also Goleman, Boyatzis, and McKee, *Primal Leadership*; Goleman, *Social Intelligence*.

their lives, or, at least, not the anticipated degree of change—not enough "bang for the buck."

Something crucial is missing from the two-step approach.[4] To be sure, these two steps capture critically important elements, but much more needs to happen besides "knowing" and "doing" for true spiritual growth to happen.

Have you ever noticed how, when you actually get to the point of trying to put into practice something you have learned, it doesn't feel quite the same as it did when you were first imagining yourself doing it? Like the problem of New Year's resolutions, when we make them, they seem so important and relevant. We imagine ourselves successfully keeping them and we anticipate the good feelings associated with the desired outcome. In practice, however, they turn out to be harder to do than they seemed in our imagination. Discouragement easily ensues. If we had a more robust and biblically sound view of learning—that it includes the whole heart (dispositions, desires, emotions)—we would experience more fruit in spiritual growth.

Let's try a common example to illustrate this, the injunction to forgive those who offend or harm us. In the two-step approach, we first receive good teaching that explains the concept of forgiveness. Usually, it goes something like the following: to forgive means that we choose no longer to hold the offense against that person. We release him or her from the pain and penalty of the offense. We resist the temptation to use it against that person. We don't bring it up again.

We can now recite a good, solid, biblical definition of forgiveness. We can add color to the idea, such as that we can forgive someone without necessarily feeling warm and close to the offender. We can confidently say that we understand it, and we are tempted to say that we have "learned what forgiveness means." We have the first step down.

Now comes the second: application. This step turns out to be a lot harder than we imagined. We can fairly easily forgive some minor slight, but what about something that cuts us right to the core, that wounds us beyond words? You can no doubt immediately begin to think of moments

---

4. Probably a more serious problem, which I will not examine but which I will mention here, is how much Christians participate in the life of the Christian community without ever being challenged (or at least noticing the challenge) to "apply." It is easy to put the Christian life on autopilot.

in which you struggled and failed to forgive someone, even though you understood clearly what forgiveness means.

Here is an example that lives among the most painful and difficult of situations requiring forgiveness. A friend, a longtime, devoted follower of Jesus, has a daughter who has been raped. I have heard him tell the story of her assault several times, in weekend conferences with incarcerated men (he is deeply involved in prison ministry). The crime happened a long time ago, but the telling makes it feel like it was yesterday, especially since all of us dads with daughters reel in horror and fear of the prospect of its happening to ours. In the days following the crime, as my friend seethed with rage, he began working out a plan to find and kill the rapist. Keep in mind that this man was—at the time of this tragedy—a deeply committed Christian, a model to many of us. In telling the story, he goes into detail about how, with coldly rational anger, he plotted to carry out the deed. Fortunately, he did not, and over time, little bit by little bit, God taught him about forgiveness. And it involved more than just "choosing" to forgive. It required and called forth a change in his heart.

Something particularly heinous comes to light in sexual crimes: the horrible violence, the invasion of one's very person. How could we ever forgive someone for doing such an awful thing? Nonetheless, for any and all such atrocities, God calls his children to offer forgiveness.[5] Yes, it is offensive to write such words. I feel the offense. But then I remember Jesus, the unblemished Lamb of God, hanging upon the cross, saying, "Father, forgive them." This is not a morality tale. It is an expression of the very heart of God that we—as followers of Christ—are called to emulate. This is Christianity for grownups.

Let's back up from such a soul-searing example to something more common in day-to-day experience. Within Christian circles we regularly hear stories about church fights. Perhaps you have witnessed or participated in one. People feel very strongly about some matter and they go after each other in order to achieve their aims. In heated arguments, people say things hurtful to each other. As the Apostle Paul said, we "bite and devour" (Gal 5:15) one another for all manner of perceived slights. People on the receiving end of such treatment go away and rehearse and rehash the hurtful words, in disbelief that so-and-so said such and such

5. Certainly, crimes should be tried and dealt with according to the full extent of the law. By talking about forgiveness, I am not suggesting that we should forego any legal consequence. Forgiveness is a matter apart from application of the law.

a thing. Here, too, Christ calls for people to forgive. We cannot take back the hurtful things said. The only way forward is the way of forgiveness. Again: Christianity for grownups.

If you've ever struggled with applying some principle of discipleship, you know exactly how difficult it is. We often cannot make the application until we've taken time to examine the contents of our own hearts and to wrestle with what we find there. In the case of forgiveness, for example, we might need to admit the spirit of vengeance and self-righteous assertion that we find there. We might have to admit that we get much pleasure from nursing the grudge and playing the victim. Sometimes these attitudes and feelings are hard to discern, because they so thoroughly mix with the legitimate feeling of pain from the wounds of the offense. Separating out and feeling the wounds without allowing vengefulness and bitterness to take root is a spiritual challenge that the two-step does not adequately address. It takes work at self-awareness and an openness to follow the way of Christ.

THE BIBLE'S DESCRIPTION OF "HEART"?

While accepting the importance of both understanding and application, hopefully we also can see that what I have called the two-step reflects a naïve, impoverished view of human nature very common among Christians today. This view, in my opinion, contributes to frustration and confusion among believers and stunts their growth. To help remedy this situation requires frankly acknowledging the hard work ahead of us. Let's begin by examining the biblical concept of "heart," and then look at how it relates to current research exploring the link between emotions and thought.

The Hebrew word for "heart" is *leb*. The main Greek (New Testament) word is *kardia*. We recognize this word most easily in our medical and exercise terms like "cardio" and "cardiologist." *Leb* and *kardia* cover the same territory, so we will take them together because of the consistency in usage across the Old and New Testaments. Keep in mind, they both identify the *totality* of a person: thoughts, feelings, attitudes, dispositions, and choices. Biblically speaking, your heart *is you*, all of you.[6] I want to emphasize that this biblical view encompasses the intellect as well as the

6. And is a matter of deep concern for God's care of humans. In 1 Sam 16:7, God leads Samuel to choose David for Israel's leader. People look on the outward appearance, but the Lord looks on the heart.

emotions. Under the term *leb* in a Hebrew lexicon, you will find these words: mind, will, understanding, thought, attention, imagination, reflection, memory, intention, determination,[7] *as well as* the complex phenomena we call emotions. The same can be said for *kardia* in a Greek lexicon.

Taking this comprehensive description of "heart," then, what does it do for our understanding of spiritual maturity? It demands that to grow to maturity, we must pay attention to all the heart's dimensions.

Let's look at one of the anchor points of the Old Testament, the Shema of Deut 6:4–5: "Hear, O Israel: The Lord is our God, the Lord alone. You shall love the Lord your God with all your heart and with all your soul, and with all your might." This is the greatest of all commandments in the Torah. To love God according to this verse means quite literally to love God with complete devotion, without reserve of any kind. It is total and all-encompassing. The same command appears in Matt 22:37–40, in which a Pharisee questions Jesus about the greatest commandment. Jesus quotes the Shema and adds the second greatest commandment, from Lev 19:18: "You shall love the Lord, your God, with all your heart, and with all your soul, and with all your mind. And the second is like it: You shall love your neighbor as yourself."[8]

These two places in Scripture are well known. That we are called to love God and neighbor is undisputed among Christians, but why does it matter so much that we love as the Bible commands? In other words, how seriously do we need to try to fulfill these commands? To answer these questions takes us straight to fundamental convictions about human nature and the life of faith. Loving God wholeheartedly relates directly to the way we are created and to the aim of serving God's mission in the world.

Remember that the Shema in Deuteronomy comes in the context of the identity and mission of God's people, Israel. They were called to be, according to Exod 19:5–6, a "kingdom of priests and a holy nation." Their

---

7. See, for example, the *Brown-Driver-Briggs Hebrew and English Lexicon*, 524–25. This book is a reprint of the original 1906 edition. For explanation of the New Testament term, one standard reference work is Kittel, *Theological Dictionary of the New Testament*. See 3:611–13. These pages show especially clearly the three-dimensional aspect of the heart: mind, emotions, and will.

8. The attentive reader may notice that "heart" and "mind" are both mentioned, as if they refer to distinguishable aspects of a person. However, since Jesus is repeating the verse from Deuteronomy, he follows the same convention of a form of repetition by using synonyms for emphasis. "Heart" and "mind" are ways of emphasizing the whole-person call to love God and neighbor.

mission—by the ways in which they worshipped the true, living God *and* how they lived together in community with one another—was to make visible to their neighbors, "the nations," *the kind of God* they served. In so doing they would show the world that God is a God of love, power, justice, and mercy. If we want people to get an idea of what God is like, we need to demonstrate the power of God's love.

This same idea goes deeper and requires a bit of theological short-hand, at least for the moment. We all are created in God's image. If God's nature is love, then, by virtue of our being created in that image, we can—by God's grace—love in a way analogous to God's love. (The shorthand: to sketch this picture more adequately we would need a discussion of how God's grace redeems us in Christ, whose grace transforms our nature. This train of thought goes beyond our topic of creation. We will take it up in due time.) This is precisely the way the Bible describes it. That our hearts are twisted by sin and in need of forgiveness, healing, and restora-tion does not negate the fact that being created in God's image calls us to live so that people can see a little bit of what God is like through us. To embody and demonstrate God's love, then, requires the whole self—the heart—to be fully engaged.

Now, let's notice how the assumption we discussed earlier, about understanding and application, truncate the biblical concept of "heart." Because it focuses on conceptual knowing and doing, it leaves out dimen-sions of our nature (or heart) that, left unexamined, produce bad fruit. Perhaps you've heard the teaching that loving God really means obeying God, regardless of feelings. By God's grace, you can obey God even if you don't *feel like* obeying. This claim, though in one sense true, says too much. Certainly we should not equate loving God with mushy sentimen-tality without action. Admittedly, we can feel warm and close to God (or, at least an image of God), yet not do what God commands.

But that sword cuts the other direction, too. Merely obeying God's commands without feeling devoted, heartfelt attachment to God does not indicate love for God, either. It is obligation. It looks like the faith of the older son in the story of the Prodigal Son from Luke 15. No, since we are created for loving, intimate communion with God, we cannot fulfill the command to love God unless our hearts attach to God, unless they are properly ordered through and through (thoughts, desires, dispositions, etc.) according to God's creative and redemptive purposes.

Consider, likewise, what Jesus says about loving one's neighbor. (We'll leave aside for now what he says about loving enemies!) Haven't you heard it said, "You don't have to *like* someone in order to *love* him"? Again, an important truth resides in this statement, but also a dangerous falsehood, if taken too far. Our loving someone does not *require* that we always feel warm and cozy toward that person. We can love someone even when we have negative feelings, even when we're angry or upset. However, it does not follow that feelings have nothing to do with love, as if they can be ignored.[9] If I consistently feel nothing for someone that I say I love, one must certainly begin to doubt the authenticity of my claim to love. In fact, consistently to feel nothing, which usually leads to doing nothing (especially when something needs doing), suggests hatred rather than love.

To embody and put into effect the Bible's call to love God with all one's heart, therefore, we must take care not to get trapped in these two common but unhelpful and contradictory postures, either of duty without feeling or feeling without action. Rather, we need to explore again the deep connections between intellect, emotion, and will. We need to see how what we think and how we feel actually work in tandem, leading to actions we take. To gain in this way means a much richer and more fruitful life of discipleship.

LOVE: THE HEART'S ATTACHMENTS

If you spend any time at all thinking about how human nature works, you will notice, among other things, that we are created (1) to join together in relationships of various kinds and (2) to make and keep goals of various kinds. These features of human nature reveal how the heart attaches to that which we truly love.

Notice, for example, what happens when you make a new friend, how all the dimensions of the heart that we are examining come into play. First, you "get acquainted," which means typically that you become familiar with those character qualities that identify the new friend. You thus form a concept of the friend. Accompanying those thoughts (and interacting with them) are emotionally tonal attitudes like curiosity and

9. This point raises another concern, stemming from the misguided notion that *agape* love—the kind of love that God has for us, which is unconditional—refers only to the bare will. Emotions are superfluous, according to this view. Think about it: do you want your loved one to love you only with the will and without any feeling?

interest and, perhaps, growing admiration and respect. You can feel a
bond forming (the attachment) with that person, which prompts you to
desire to take actions to develop the friendship further: meals together or
some other regular activity that puts you together. In forming this friendship, your heart begins to attach to the friend in love and loyalty and
concern.

As the relationship matures, you learn the shortcomings as well as
the admirable qualities of this friend. The relationship might weather
some difficult moments. But if the friendship does endure and mature, at
some point you conclude that you love this friend. (For college students,
for example, such friendships form during college years and last for a life-
time.) Like Jonathan who loved David, your love is not prompted merely
by an act of the will. You're not "choosing" to love this friend. Your heart
is knit to theirs.

This example of friendship reveals how the heart attaches to things
we care about. If we were to take the time to examine and order all our interests and concerns, all the "objects" to which our hearts attach, we could
develop a pretty good list. With time and reflection, the items on your list
would begin to fall into an informal hierarchy. You could recognize some
choices made in relation to the people or things on your list. You could
also recognize a disposition to act toward what is on the list, a disposition that involves thoughts and feelings combined. There is tremendous
variety here, of course. Think about who and what you love: your family and friends, your church community or small group, your hobbies,
your prized possessions, your job (I hope) and co-workers, and God. Of
course, you don't love them all equally. Something takes precedence. And
the degrees of your love show up in how you make choices relative to all
these different objects of concern. When two loves conflict, you consistently choose the more important one over the others. Remember Jesus'
sage words, "No one can serve two masters."

Now, to demonstrate the integrated dimensions of the heart found
in the biblical concept (and to continue the work of seeing the connection between thoughts and feelings often lacking in Christian teaching),
consider what we stereotypically think of as the most cerebral and "intellectual" of pursuits, therefore the least emotional: the scientist working in
her lab. The stereotype is one of cool rationality, keeping emotions at bay
so as not to spoil the research. But why or how did the scientist become
a scientist in the first place? Granting that she could be motivated by a

number of external forces (for example, expectations of significant others, obligation to keep a family tradition, possibility of fame and wealth), most likely the scientist has chosen her particular field because of *interest*. And what is "interest"? It is the heart attaching to an object—the scientific research. Here we start to see that even intellectual interest has emotional tonality: curiosity, wonder, awe, even love.

We are talking here about what John Wesley and other thinkers of his generation called the "affections." We do not use this word in this way anymore, but the concept is exceedingly important and we do get close in our usage today. Its cognate surfaces when we talk about "feeling affection" toward someone with whom we have warm, connected feelings. I feel affectionate toward the students I get to know well. I feel concern for their well-being. I enjoy interacting with them. I am glad to see them appear at my office door. I hope for them a fulfilling future. Thus, my heart attaches to them, not unlike (even if to a lesser degree) a parent to a child. Notice the emotional tonality. We would not say that our scientist in the previous paragraph feels affection for her research. But, she is "affected" by it. Her heart attaches to it, showing a kind of love.

In the next section, then, I will attempt to make a turn toward theological matters and describe how emotions actually contribute to our *knowing God*. We will continue to refer to thought, but because this angle of vision on emotions has been largely ignored, I will concentrate on how emotions and thoughts work together. I am therefore talking about "head knowledge" and "heart knowledge" as one single mental-emotional act. This idea, upon first look, may seem odd, even impossible. For the next few paragraphs, I beg the reader's patience as I try to describe a characteristic that I believe is of utmost importance for spiritual growth, but it involves entering probably unfamiliar academic territory.

USING CONTEMPORARY RESEARCH ON EMOTIONS TO THINK ABOUT OUR SPIRITUAL LIVES

For roughly the past twenty years, scholars have been exploring the link between emotions and thought. Some now argue that emotions actually help do epistemic work ("epistemic" is the philosophers' term for what counts as knowledge).

This line of thinking represents a significant change from earlier generations of scholars. William James, one of the fathers of modern psychology, posited that emotions were the physiological reactions we have to emotion-inducing situations, reactions like the hair on the back of the neck standing up or the skin becoming clammy. This view held sway for many years. In contrast to this physicalist view, some scholars now argue for what is called a cognitive understanding of emotions. That is, emotions contribute to the work of thinking. Scholars of this ilk use terms like "evaluative judgments"[10] or "concern-based construals"[11] to attempt to describe the link between emotions and thought. They argue, for example, that an emotion is more than a feeling. It is "about" something. Emotions attach to objects.

Because of the older way of thinking about emotions, we have tended to view them with suspicion. Emotions contribute to irrational responses. They cause problems. We readily acknowledge that emotions *can* create problems, but, properly trained (and this is an important condition), they also contribute to good thinking.

Many of us remember Spock from *Star Trek*, the Vulcan with no emotions. Spock represents the pessimistic view of emotions that we inherited from the rationalism of the Enlightenment. Yet Dylan Evans has argued that Spock's "Vulcan morality" would actually have made him dumber than the humans who turned to Spock for his calm logic in crisis situations, in precisely those moments that we think of as needing cool heads. Without properly trained emotions, Spock could not have made "rational" decisions.[12]

So, what do emotions do that contributes to sound thinking? First, they narrow our attention—our cognitive focus—to the object(s) of concern. This narrowing produces heightened awareness and sharper concentration. Emotions draw attention to what really needs attention in that particular moment. Some theorists refer to this function of emotions as the "quick and dirty" work so important when time is short and a decision must be made. But the "quick and dirty" work is not the only way emotions contribute to sound thinking. They also help notice features of an object of concern that evoke certain emotions. In other words, certain properties of an object correlate with certain emotional responses. This point is especially significant for considering spiritual maturity.

10. See, for example, Nussbaum, *Upheavals of Thought*, and Helm, *Emotional Reason*.
11. See, for example, Roberts, *Spiritual Emotions*.
12. Evans, *The Science of Sentiment*, 64.

To make sense of this idea, I need to introduce two notions that I have grabbed from philosophers: (1) "salience"[13] and (2) "import" or "concern."[14] A salient property is some feature of an object that *stands out* to our perception as a key feature of the object. An object of import is something of value, something about which we feel strong concern. (Remember, "object" here can mean person as well as something non-personal.) The feeling is *about* something—some feature of the object of import. We *care* about it *because* it has value.

Let's connect this cognitive view of emotions to our experience with God. We understand from Scripture that we are created *to know* God. I am using the word *know* both in the technical philosophical (epistemological) sense as well as in the biblical sense, to experience God personally and intimately. As beings created in God's image, we have both capacity and desire for relationship with God. God created our hearts to attach— to God. To use the philosophers' language, God is an object of import. In fact, God presents himself to us as the Ultimate Object.[15] Through the gracious work of the Holy Spirit, God *prompts and initiates* the feeling of desire for God as well as the *awareness* of God in our thoughts and experiences.[16] We can know God because God comes to us.

Furthermore, and very important for our thinking about spiritual maturity, in getting to know God we experience the "salient features" of God's nature that evoke emotionally tonal thoughts. By the term "emotionally tonal," I am seeking to point to that integrated phenomenon of thoughts that have feeling tone, even though we may not recognize them as emotions. In the book *Perceiving God*, philosopher William Alston recounts the experiences of a number of people describing their perceptions

13. I'm taking the idea of "salience" from the works of Elgin and DeSousa in Brun, Doguoglu, and Kuenzle, *Epistemology and Emotions*.

14. Two philosophers, discussing the same phenomena but using different terms, are Bennet Helm, who explains "import" in *Emotional Reason*, 32. Baylor University philosopher Robert C. Roberts calls emotions "concern-based construals." See his *Spiritual Emotions*.

15. Remember, God is clearly Subject, first. As I noted in a previous footnote, "object" does not, with reference to God, reduce to something we can manipulate. To use the language of Martin Buber, I am not talking about an I-It relationship, but an I-Thou relationship, even though I'm following philosophers' use of the word "object."

16. For a strong description of how divine revelation works with human experience, see Abraham, *Crossing the Threshold of Divine Revelation*. See also his more recent work, *Aldersgate and Athens*.

of God. Their stories include words that point to God's "salient features," like "good," "loving," "compassionate," "wise" and "glorious."[17] Notice the response-evoking emotional tonality of the terms. One of the supremely salient features (if not the supreme feature) of God's nature is love. When we know God's love, we feel that love. This is why the command to love God must mean more than dutifully obeying God. As 1 John says, we love God because God first loved us.

Notice also that the terms people used to describe their perception of God include cognitive content. We can take the proposition, "God is good," and analyze it. (Notice how this process looks like what we normally think of as "theology.") We can think of "good" in terms of "morally good" or in terms of "beneficent," for example. "Morally good" evokes thoughts of God's holiness. "Beneficent" prompts thoughts of God's providential care. Notice that if we take these terms as salient features of God's nature and if our emotions are appropriately tuned, the terms evoke an emotionally tonal thought, not a merely intellectual thought. To state that 1 John verse in a slightly more philosophical-sounding way, therefore, God presents himself to us as loving and we find ourselves drawn to love God in response.

This discussion of the deep connection in our minds between thoughts and feelings shows us how the heart actually works and it matches the scriptural description. Knowing and loving God has both cognitive and emotional content.[18] But there is actually one more step that involves the disposition to act. If, for example, (1) God communicates love to us and (2) we feel love for God in return, then (3) that love expresses itself in something we could call loyalty, and loyalty shows itself in visible behavior. Loving God supremely means serving God in daily life. It leads to choices and actions that match our hearts' disposition.[19]

Some readers may object that I've taken a too-rosy view of the heart in the foregoing description. Let me acknowledge, therefore, that the heart can resist the work of God and get twisted out of shape. We can quench and grieve the Spirit. Our love for God can grow cold. Our desires and attachments can be disordered. In fact, when we talk about original

17. Alston, *Perceiving God*, 12–20.

18. This point has important implications for Christian doctrine, which we will examine in a later chapter.

19. A full account of this matter requires our thinking about how the heart's loyalty is diverted and distorted by sin. We'll have to leave that topic for another time.

sin or the sin nature, we could think of disordered desire (or affections) as the flip side of disbelief. Rather than aiming our affections at God, we aim them at lesser objects of love. This disordering produces a number of unhappy consequences, which we know well. The point I would like to make here is that the cognitive view of emotions holds from this angle, as well. Thought and emotion go together. If the heart is disordered, then the understanding is adversely affected. Misshapen dispositions lead to wrong actions. When the heart is out of order, everything about a person is negatively affected.

This exploration of contemporary research calls to mind observations that some of our spiritual forebears—who understood the deep connection between the contours of the heart and the Christian life—have made. We can learn much from them. John Wesley has made an especially important contribution to our thinking precisely because he understood the link between heart and life. As I mentioned a few paragraphs back, Wesley used the word *affections*—as the thinkers of his day commonly did[20]—to refer to the heart's attachments. As I understand their use of this term (and others like "holy tempers"), I see a helpful parallel between Wesley's ideas and the contemporary research.

JOHN WESLEY AND THE HEART

John Wesley and his brother, Charles, are well known in history for forming and leading a movement known as Methodism. Today, millions of Christians around the world, in distinct but historically related denominations,[21] are heirs to the Wesleys. In wider Christian circles, John is known far more for his preaching and organizing abilities (and his dedication and discipline) than for his ideas, even though at least two recent generations of scholars have produced significant writings that demonstrate the weightiness of Wesley's theology. With regard to

20. Jonathan Edwards, eighteenth-century American pastor, theologian, and college president (still regarded by some people as America's greatest theologian), made copious observations about the affections, both religious and otherwise, in a book titled, *The Religious Affections*. The book was first published in 1746, and, although our understanding of psychology has changed, it still holds many wonderful insights into the human heart.

21. For a helpful survey of these connections among denominations that most people would not recognize as having any such relationship, see Knight, *From Aldersgate to Azusa Street*.

teaching on the Christian life, Wesley's work is particularly important. I hope, with the present work, to help people—both inside and outside of Methodism—see the value of his teaching. I think it is particularly telling and relevant in light of the recent research on the emotions that I just sketched.

To get at the core of Wesley's teachings, a brief telling of a significant part of his story is necessary. In his Journal, he describes his youthful understanding of the Christian faith as "not being so bad as other people, having a kindness for religion and reading the Bible, going to church and saying my prayers."[22] He sincerely, yet superficially, went through the motions of religious observance, while the heart's particular yearnings aimed elsewhere. Sound familiar?

Then, at age twenty-two (1725), he encountered Thomas a Kempis' book *Christian Pattern* (known today as *The Imitation of Christ*), which set him on a different trajectory. Of this work Wesley wrote, "I began to see that true religion [i.e., true Christian faith] was seated in the heart, and that God's law extended to all our thoughts as well as words and actions."

Notice how new thoughts—in response to his reading—gave impetus to a new vision. That vision is accompanied by a new (or at least modified) set of desires. This change in understanding provoked a longing for experiential appropriation of this new vision. Subsequently, for thirteen years, from 1725 until 1738, Wesley worked hard to make this new belief about true Christian faith true in his experience (his feelings). He even came to America as a missionary, desiring to (by his own account) save his own soul and share the Gospel with Native Americans. According to his testimony over this period of time, he lacked consistently (although feeling it occasionally) the "spiritual emotions"—to use Robert Roberts' term—of an authentic Christian life. For example, he lacked confidence (notice the emotional tone of "confidence") that he personally knew God's love and forgiveness.[23] In his work as a priest in Georgia, and during his return to England, he was acutely aware that he did not consistently *feel* as

22. If a reader would like to see the whole account, it can be found in *The Works of John Wesley*, 18:242–50.

23. Notice again the salient feature—forgiveness. God is a forgiving God. The believer's emotional response, when the heart is properly tuned, is to feel the benefit of God's forgiveness. There is emotional tonality to the experience of forgiveness that goes along with both God's nature and God's presenting that forgiving nature to us in the act of forgiving.

the Bible describes the Christian life, therefore he was not confident that he was a real Christian. He rigorously observed religious duties, but he did not know the love of God that chases away fear.

For this reason, many students of Wesley have seen May 24, 1738—his Aldersgate experience—as a critical turning point. Wesley tells the story this way: "In the evening I went very unwillingly to a society in Aldersgate Street, where one was reading Luther's Preface to the Epistle to the Romans. About a quarter before nine, while he was describing the change which God works in the heart through faith in Christ, I felt my heart strangely warmed. I felt I did trust in Christ, Christ alone for salvation, and an assurance was given me that he had taken away *my* sins, even *mine*, and saved *me* from the law of sin and death"[24] (italics in the original).

In 1725 and in 1738, as well as other points that we could identify from Wesley's Journal, we see the heart at work, and it combines thoughts—sometimes specifically theological ruminations (with implications for the role of doctrine in shaping the heart)—accompanied by changes in desires, which, in turn, lead to goal-driven behaviors. If we were to study the full account of Wesley's testimony, we would see this deep interaction of the heart's dimensions very clearly, but the truth is, we could find expressions of this multidimensional work of the heart in many testimonies of faith, past and present, including our own.

Wesley carried certain basic convictions regarding the nature of the heart in relation to Christian discipleship throughout his long ministry. Because of that emphasis, people outside the Wesleyan tradition (and, frankly, many people within it!) have not had much opportunity to explore Wesley's most compelling teaching regarding the Christian life. Whereas virtually all Wesley scholars acknowledge that he was not a systematic theologian in the usual academic way we think of such persons, Wesley's theology of the Christian life ("soteriology," to use the academic term) is nuanced and rich. Given what we noted earlier in relation to a cognitive view of emotions, his doctrines look fresh and timely today.

Wesley's major work on the subject of spiritual maturity is called "A Plain Account of Christian Perfection." (Don't get stuck on the word *perfection.* As we have noted, it does not mean flawless, but rather, mature, realizing God's aim.) He referred to this doctrine as the "grand

24. *The Works of John Wesley,* 18:249–50.

depositum" for which God had called Methodists into existence. In other words, he saw it as Methodism's particular contribution to the renewal of the church.[25] "A Plain Account" is absolutely laced with "heart" talk. Wesley writes, for example, that one of the best ways to describe Christian maturity is as "love governing the heart, running through all our tempers, words and actions." Notice the "governance" language and, likewise, what it governs. Randy Maddox says that, by "tempers," Wesley meant the enduring, habitual dispositions that show a person's character in the actions they typically take.[26]

Tempers, therefore, are shaped by—to use that philosophical language again—objects of import, what we habitually desire (or fear) and think about. Tempers are shaped as well as by the habits (disciplines) we practice.[27] And tempers clearly have that emotional tonality that I have been stressing. As we grow toward maturity, then, every aspect of our heart must come to our attention for assessment. In the following comments from "A Plain Account," I have put in italics words with emotional tone:

> Christian perfection [maturity] is the *loving* God with all our heart, mind, soul and strength. This implies that no wrong *temper* [attitude, disposition, with feelings], none contrary to *love*, remains in the soul.[28]
>
> All our *tempers*, and thoughts, and words, and works, spring from *love*.[29]
>
> The perfection I hold, '*Love rejoicing* evermore, praying without ceasing, and in everything giving thanks . . . '[30]

25. This comment can be found in Wesley's letter to Robert Carr Brackenbury, written in 1790. See Telford, *The Letters of John Wesley*, 8:237–238, or Jackson, *The Works of John Wesley*, 13:9. You can see how important the doctrine was to Wesley—and should be to us! For the full text of "A Plain Account," see Wesley, *The Works of John Wesley*, 11:366–446.

26. Maddox, *Responsible Grace*, 70.

27. For anyone interested in a full, scholarly description of this point, see Clapper, *John Wesley on Religious Affections*. A much more accessible work of Dr. Clapper's is his *As if the Heart Mattered*.

28. Wesley, "A Plain Account," 394.

29. Ibid., 417.

30. Ibid., 418.

[God] is their one *desire,* their one *delight,* and they are *continually happy* in him. They *love* their neighbour as themselves. They *feel* as sincere, fervent, constant a *desire* for the *happiness* of every man, good or bad, friend or enemy, as for their own.[31]

God's action prompts a response consistent with God's nature, involving thoughts, desires, and motives. As the heart engages with God's work over a period of time, we see thoughts and feelings coalesce into dispositions (or "tempers"), which, remember, are tendencies to act in certain ways. Thoughts and actions in the Christian life that reflect God's purposes are consistently[32] colored by the holy tempers reflective of God's nature. This point is crucial for understanding Wesley's teaching on spiritual maturity.

Wesley therefore claims in "A Plain Account" that the Christian's blessed privilege is consistently to feel the joy and happiness attending to the love of God that the Holy Spirit pours into our hearts. Scattered throughout this treatise are abundant references to peace, joy, humility, confidence, liberty, and comfort. The religious affections shaped by grace over time will produce holy tempers—visible evidence of the character qualities that emulate Christ himself. As Wesley said it, happiness and holiness are inherently connected (two ideas we hardly ever get together in our modern context), giving the normative Christian life both a moral and missional, as well as emotional, tone. If we want to grow to maturity, we must do more than work at believing the right things and doing the right things. We can check the emotional tones associated with our believing and doing to see if they reflect the heart of Christ.

How in the world is this exalted standard even possible for Christians? The short answer is God's grace (we will try to correct some frustratingly persistent misconceptions of this doctrine in a subsequent chapter), but let me turn to another of Wesley's sermons, "On Working Out Our Own Salvation" (based on Phil 2:12–13), for a more substantive one. In this sermon, Wesley emphasizes that the *motive* and *energy* for our commitment to maturity comes from the Spirit of God. The Philippians verse

---

31. Ibid.

32. We must always include a caveat when talking about feelings and the Christian life. We do not have to wait until we feel a certain way in order to act. Nor is there something wrong with the action if, when we act, we do not feel the expected feelings. The point I am trying to make here reflects the emotional impact of the work of God over time, not necessarily in any given moment. We can reasonably expect—over time—that the emotional tones that characterize our lives will show more and more the nature of Christ.

states that we work out our salvation *for (because)* God is at work in us. Wesley writes, "God breathes into us every good desire, and brings every good desire to good effect."[33] The work of grace (the activity of the Holy Spirit) evokes *the right kinds of desires* (that match God's purposes) and the energy to fulfill those desires. *Because* God is at work, then we *can* work.

This truth is double-edged. On the one hand, it offers a serious challenge. We cannot legitimately settle for a low shelf spirituality that allows excuses for immaturity. It takes commitment, sustained effort, even courage. But on the other hand, we don't have to gin up the energy and motivation ourselves. A faithful, gracious God provides what we need.

SOME IMPLICATIONS FOR SPIRITUAL MATURITY

The material we have covered in this chapter, from the Bible's description of the heart to John Wesley's teaching, probably raises certain questions. First, you may be wondering, does God really care that much about our feelings? The answer is an enthusiastic "yes!"—with qualifications. Surely God is not overly concerned to protect our feelings as if to make sure we always feel secure and comfortable. Nonetheless, when we study the Scriptures, we see how often emotionally tonal words attend to the work of God. God's Spirit provides comfort, confidence, and peace. We can feel peace in the face of trouble, hope for the future rather than despair, and confidence in God's presence no matter what the circumstance. These emotionally tonal qualities come from having our hearts' dispositions shaped by engaging with God over time.

Furthermore and more importantly, we share feelings *for others* that Jesus demonstrates: compassion for the afflicted, love for the lost and lonely, anger about injustice and so on. Remember, following John Wesley, we are not talking about mere feelings that can come and go, but about long-term persistent "affections" that evoke Christ-like attitudes and behaviors. In short, God cares about the emotional tonality of our lives because they demonstrate the life that God makes available to followers of Jesus. Our affections are not just for us, but also for others.

A second idea follows: by God's grace, *our desires and feelings can change.* This point is absolutely crucial for understanding spiritual

33. Wesley, "On Working Out Our Own Salvation," in *The Works of John Wesley,* 3:199–209.

maturity. We're called to grow in the knowledge and love of God and neighbor. If spiritual maturity means having the mind of Christ and walking as he walked, then our attitudes and actions need to change to come into alignment with his. Our feelings can change. We can (and must) grow emotionally as part of growing spiritually. Our emotions (affections) can be trained through sound teaching and through the practices of the faith. Thereby the Holy Spirit transforms us, reorienting our desires and aiming them at the things of God.

If spiritual maturity means embodying the attitudes and actions of Jesus, then the Bible's many descriptions of Jesus' attitudes and actions in particular situations become guides for what we should seek for in our own lives. One of the most powerful challenges for me, personally, is to ponder Jesus' response to the leper in Matthew 8 and Luke 5. The leper, breaking the law by even walking along a public road (much less being near other people), confronts Jesus and pleads, "Lord, if you are willing, you can make me clean." While acknowledging Jesus' full divinity, keep in mind also his full humanity. It is very easy for us to miss the emotional quality of this story if we focus only on the divine power in Jesus to heal the leper.

Imagine Jesus standing in front of this diseased man. The Law of Moses required lepers—regardless of the severity of their condition—to separate themselves from the rest of society. If they saw anybody walking along a path or road, they had to cry out "Unclean!" in order to let the oncoming person know that a leper is present. The person could then keep a healthy (and I do mean healthy) distance.[34] For a leper to get too close was a breach of the law and a health danger. Surely all these thoughts were going through Jesus' mind in this moment. Yet, without speaking a word, Jesus *first reached out and touched the leper*, then said, "I am willing. Be made clean."

Why in the world did Jesus touch this guy? I imagine the fully human Jesus at precisely this point. He has the power of God to heal and he knows it. He did not have to touch this man! Jesus knew the law and undoubtedly felt at least some repugnance at the man's condition. If it is hard for you to imagine Jesus feeling disgust, just picture yourself touching

34. The word *leprosy* in biblical times covered a wide range of conditions, all the way from psoriasis to Hansen's Disease (what we usually think of when we hear the word *leper*). Hansen's Disease is the most dangerous and deforming.

dry, scaly, cracked, oozing, bleeding skin (I apologize). And Jesus touched him anyway!

At that very moment, Jesus made himself unclean according to the law. Why did he do it? Because his loving heart was broken for this man's condition. It brings tears to my eyes, just thinking about what Jesus did. It also makes me think of 2 Cor 5:21, "For our sake he made him *to be sin who knew no sin,* so that in him we might become the righteousness of God." Can we see the extent to which God will go to save us? In making the man clean, Jesus made himself unclean. But, the point is, the man went away clean! Oh, how he must have rejoiced at this new condition.

There is a parable here for all of us. Although this story doesn't use the word *compassion,* clearly Jesus feels it for this man. Jesus couldn't keep his hands off this poor, broken soul! If Christian maturity means demonstrating the character of Christ, loving what Jesus loves, then in this story I see what Jesus ultimately expects of me, his follower. I am ashamed by my shallow self-absorptions. But, I can change. And you can, too.

We are now ready to give attention to the growth that can take place as we spend time worshipping, studying, sharing our hearts with one another, and serving in the name of Christ. It will help us, therefore, to examine some common features of the experience of growth and how God acts in these experience categories. By plotting some of the Christian life's markers—and the attitudes and actions that attend them—we gain a clearer vision of the goal (maturity) as well as some of the steps along the way.

3 The Trajectory of Christian Maturity

I am a creature of a day, passing through life as an arrow through the air.[1]

In the evening I met the believers and strongly exhorted them to "go on to perfection." To many of them it seemed a new doctrine. However, they all received it in love, and a flame was kindled which I trust neither men nor devils shall ever be able to quench.[2]

PLANNING TO GROW

In the first chapter I made mention of the Kansas State University football program and the tremendous turnaround Coach Bill Snyder engineered. Now let me return to another part of that story, but, if you don't like football, don't worry. It's not about football.

In addition to developing winning teams, Coach Snyder has become famous for his leadership and influence among other coaches. The "family tree" among currently active head coaches who spent time on Snyder's staff is impressive. Many of them credit the experience they had working with him as a significant factor in their own coaching success. For this reason people have grown interested in what Snyder has to say about leadership. One of his key principles calls for planning to improve.[3] In order to get better, you have to plan to get better. Improvement takes more

1. Wesley, "Preface to the Sermons," in *The Works of John Wesley*, 1:104–5.
2. Wesley, *The Works of John Wesley*, 21:313. The internal quote is from Heb 6:1.
3. See Shoop, Scott, and Snyder, *Leadership: Lessons from Bill Snyder*, 38–39.

than activity. Most importantly, your plan needs to demonstrate that you see how your plan helps you improve—each day.

This point seems a little circular and maybe even self-evident, but it is not. Many Christians engage in various spiritual growth activities, apparently assuming that the activity itself produces growth. Perhaps because of theological beliefs—perhaps even because of convictions I uphold in this book—we assume that any spiritual growth activity produces growth. This is not necessarily the case. If we do not keep the goal of growth toward maturity active, then religious practices can be pleasant, enjoyable, and meaningful without necessarily inducing new growth. That we can "please the flesh" while engaging in "spiritual" (religious) activities makes for one of the Christian life's big ironies.

When it comes to growth toward maturity, many (most?) Christians do not have a plan. Consequently, they do not know how to gauge growth. To be sure, they engage in activities, lots of them. In fact, one of the paradoxes of modern American Christian life is how busy people are. But for all the activity, we seem not to know what we're aiming at with regard to spiritual maturity. We need a plan.[4]

To help develop such a plan, we need a general description of the Christian life that provides reference points by which we can evaluate ourselves. I call these reference points the trajectory of Christian (or spiritual) maturity. The trajectory can work like a template or schema. It does not dictate anyone's particular experience, but it does help us recognize threshold moments that, in turn, assist in gauging how we are doing in growth toward maturity.

THE TRAJECTORY OF THE CHRISTIAN LIFE

In the preface to the Standard Sermons, John Wesley wrote, "I am a creature of a day, passing through life as an arrow through the air."[5] I like this image of movement toward the target, even though in real life, discipleship is much less linear than the arrow metaphor suggests. The word *trajectory* indicates *movement toward* the aim that God intends for

4. Having a plan does not suggest a lack of trust in God's work, nor does it imply mere human effort. We constantly depend on God's grace for the ability to undertake this challenge ("grace" will occupy our attention in the next chapter). Assuming God's grace at work to help us grow, every Christian and every Christian group should have a plan for growth.

5. Wesley, *The Works of John Wesley*, 1:104.

people, even if the trajectory is twisty and uneven at times. I am following Wesley's description of, as scholars call it, the *via salutis*—the way of
salvation—the contours of the Christian life.[6]

A selection of Wesley's Sermons provides the marker points on the
trajectory of spiritual maturity. They plot the movements from one's condition prior to knowing and following Jesus right through to full-blown
spiritual adulthood. Following Wesley, then, I will use the words "asleep,"
"awake" (or "awakened"), "faith and new birth" (also "conversion"), and
then, departing from Wesley's terms, I will use "mature/maturing disciple" to describe what Wesley called alternatively "holiness," "sanctification," and "Christian perfection." One can see from these latter terms the
source for some of the controversy between Calvinists and Wesleyans,
particularly "Christian perfection." For this reason I have chosen (hopefully) more acceptable terms in order to make the case for spiritual maturity—our primary concern (which was also Wesley's)—without getting
entangled in debates that do not materially affect the purpose of this book.

"Asleep"

I remember, as a boy, practicing the piano for the parentally legislated
thirty minutes a day. For thirty minutes I plodded away, robotically working through the scale exercises and the pieces I would have to play for the
teacher in the weekly lesson. My hands were going through the motions,
but my heart was completely detached from the activity. I may have been
physically sitting at the piano, but inwardly I was already outside playing
baseball. With regard to the goal of my becoming an accomplished piano
player, I was dead asleep.

Charles Wesley wrote a sermon titled, "Awake, Thou That Sleepest,"
that parallels for the spiritual life what I experienced as a piano player. It
describes the condition of humanity's "natural state"[7] apart from living
faith in Christ. "Asleep" means something like, "unaware of God's special
and particular claim on one's life."

Prior to conscious faith in Christ, most people live in a general state
of unawareness of God's intense and particular interest in them and,

6. Scholars use the Latin phrase *ordo salutis* (order of salvation) or *via salutis* (way of
salvation). We are simply talking about the divine guidelines and impulses by which the
Christian life is lived.

7. Wesley, *The Works of John Wesley*, 1:142.

likewise, of their accountability to God. Generally, an "asleep" person seems entirely content[8] with life as it is, or perhaps assumes that the way one lives is the way life is meant to be, even if he or she feels scattered moments of spiritual yearning or loneliness or has twinges of moral anxiousness. Such a person may express sincere belief in God, may consider herself or himself a Christian, and may have a connection to a church fellowship. Circumstances vary widely but the basic condition exhibits a lack of awareness of God's claims on one's life, hence the appropriateness of the term "asleep."

People who are asleep might be very morally upright or they might be "happy sinners." The morally upright may live with integrity and may even think of themselves as religious and may very well be. They may be very active in their churches. The "happy sinner," on the other hand, seems not to worry about such things. Since I work with college students, the easy example for the "happy sinner" is the "party animal," the student who seems able to live in an almost completely debauched way without any trace or twinge of tender conscience.

However a person's spiritual condition may look to us from the outside, we must exercise extreme caution in drawing conclusions about them, because God works in people's lives in a whole range of ways that are not apparent to us (or to themselves, for that matter). The key point here is that one's heart has not yet quickened or awakened to the working of God's Spirit even though the Spirit is actively working, preparing, and wooing that person toward living faith. The means by which the Spirit does this work are virtually limitless and are suited to each person's particular situation and concerns.

Let us try to imagine the combined thoughts, dispositions, and motives of one who is asleep. Imagine what this person thinks about, what gets their best attention. In other words, what is happening in this person's heart? Whatever dreams and desires this person has will rule and govern thoughts, feelings, motives, and actions. I think it was the Methodist missionary E. Stanley Jones who said, "Whatever has your attention has you." The heart of one who is asleep is captivated so comprehensively by

8. My use of "content" does not imply that people who are asleep never have problems or do not experience moments of despair, depression, or discouragement. It does mean that, with regard to their relationship to God, they manifest no awareness of God's claim on them or any sustained interest in knowing God at this level.

something other than God that this person seems not to notice God's heart and concern for them.

It is very easy for church members to impugn the motives of people who are asleep. I hear far too much from frustrated leaders trying to get some program off the ground, who say things like, "They just don't *want to*" (fill in the blank with some activity) or "They just don't *care* about . . ." We must guard against falling into this trap of judging others' motives. It hardens *our hearts* toward such people and we easily slip into sin against God and neighbor. Ironic, isn't it? While we're focused on what we think is the bad motive or lack of interest in others, *we* are the ones doing the sinning. God works graciously in unseen ways, even in those who are asleep. It is a good reminder for us to hold our tongues and guard our own hearts.

John Wesley taught that God's grace works in a person long before that person is aware that God has any interest. He called that work "prevenient grace,"[9] God's Spirit striving with one's work prior to, *coming before* (the literal meaning of "prevenient grace"), conscious openness to God's work. Experientially, this divine action can manifest itself in endless ways: in the teenager who begins to question whether God actually exists; in the flood of joy one feels at the birth of one's baby; in the heartfelt promise of a friend to pray in time of need. That teenager may look like a slacker to me. He may exhibit all the signs of irritating adolescence, yet God is at work in the very questions the teenager is asking.

Likewise, God's prevenient grace works through difficult and dangerous moments. The person who is "asleep"[10] probably will not recognize those moments at the times they occur, but later, in the awakening or perhaps after conversion or at some point further down the path, they will look back and realize, "Ah, yes, the Lord was definitely at work in me then." Prevenient grace indicates just how much God is determined to reach people with divine (*agape*) love, to transform their hearts and set

---

9. "Prevenient" derives from a Latin word, *praevenire*; the prefix, *prae*, means "before," and *venire* means "to come."

10. One can see in Wesley's own experience this phase of being asleep. By his own description, Wesley was only moderately engaged in Christian practices until 1725 (age twenty-two). As a teenage boy and early college student, Wesley said his prayers and was morally upright and observed the standard practices of the church, but he was—by his own description—asleep to the deep, transforming work that God works in hungry people's lives.

them on the path of salvation. Picturing the Christian life as a trajectory, we have our first point on the line.

One caution: A visual aid of this sort seems abstract. It cannot adequately picture real life. "Asleep" can cover an extended period of time, and it certainly does not mean that a person is never sensitive to or aware of spiritual matters. We can be episodically responsive or aware of hunger for God, but in general we are spiritually dull or insensitive.

"Awake"

At some point, one "awakens" to the awareness of God's claim on his or her life. Through some means, one becomes aware of a new feeling, a new desire, perhaps to "get right with God" or to "turn my life around." We could describe this period of awakening in many ways. Usually, a person becomes aware of the need for some part of life to improve or to change in some desired way. This moment for many has triggered thinking about "getting back into church" or going the first time. It may be as simple as that, or it may be a more difficult experience: a close encounter with death, for instance. Whatever the circumstance, something changes in a person's attitude and awareness. He or she notices a new, *persistent desire* to make life spiritually better, more whole in some way. Though the desire may vary in intensity, it seems not to go away. It may start out seemingly to have nothing to do with religion or it may be an explicit turning toward religion.

Notice how awakening to desire for God necessarily involves the whole person, the heart, as we described it in the previous chapter. With awakening comes new desire, a new set of orienting preoccupations that involve at least in part thinking about one's life. Notice, too, that when one engages in this kind of thought, one thinks those thoughts through background beliefs, or, in the case of one awakening to God's claim, may be reexamining some cherished beliefs in light of new desires. The point here is that we can see intellectual or theological work happening, even if the person engaging in such thought may not recognize this theological thinking as such. New desires coupled with this reflection often evoke new motives to do something to satisfy the new hunger.

The awakening can be dramatic and emotional or it can be subtle and incremental. John Wesley's awakening, as we noted earlier, began through reading certain books that his parents recommended while he was a college student. In one sense, therefore, this awakening is always a matter of a process, even if the actual threshold moment of awakening is very dramatic.

Notice two important points. First, many variables peculiar to one's own context contribute to an awakening to God, the significance of which one may not notice as they happen. They are, in other words, part of the process of life, the normal, day-to-day experience. There can be, so to speak, a significant amount of crucial "lead up" experience prior to the awakening. Nonetheless, secondly, there is some moment of dawning awareness in which a mental shift takes place and one becomes *aware* of the different basic orientation toward life. This awakening is a threshold moment, a conversion of sorts.

Let me offer a contemporary example from my work with college students. Ron (not his real name) was the classic, happy-go-lucky party boy. (He is the source of my "happy sinner" terminology.) Ron did well enough academically, though he was not regarded as a particularly ambitious student. For the first two years of his college experience, he basically lived for the pleasures that college freedoms afford. He enjoyed more than his share of "adult beverages," long before he could drink legally. He was popular with girls. In most respects he lived the college student's hedonistic dream. So far as anyone could tell, with regard to the trajectory toward maturity, Ron was fast asleep.

And then he went home for a weekend and met a girl who mysteriously grabbed his heart in a way that no girl had ever done. Now, before some readers start playing the "strong Christian college girl leads the party animal to Christ" video in your minds, you should know that this girl was not religiously observant. Nevertheless, meeting her provoked Ron to look at his life as if with new eyes. His whole heart became engaged in evaluating his lifestyle and, in the span of a weekend, he began asking questions about his future, and the kind of person he wanted to become. Soon he had new goals, new desires and a new plan for life.

Which led to questions about his relationship with God. With time, Ron traversed the path from "asleep" to "awake." According to our trajectory, God's grace worked effectively to awaken Ron to his hunger and need for God. What critical factors led to this change? It is hard to say, but, on reflection, one awakened to God's claim could begin to put together a workable answer. It is part of the mystery of God's providence played out in human life. Whatever those factors might be, we identify the change with reference to all of the heart's dimensions: thoughts, desires, concerns, and motives that changed for Ron. Notice again a conversion of sorts, a small one, to be sure, but nonetheless real and important.

This dawning awareness can feel clear and identifiable, as in Ron's awakening, or it can seem initially nondescript and hard to pinpoint, but growing and emerging. It also can happen as part of a very difficult time fraught with frustration and discouragement. You may know of people, for example, who have decided to get their lives "straightened out" and have made promises about changing. They set off with the best of intentions, but bottom out, perhaps several times, before finding life-changing faith in Christ.

As we think about the myriad possibilities for moments of awakening in people's lives,[11] let's ponder the crucial importance of relationships. Let's also admit that Christians can be as much a part of the problem as we are of help. If we come with a slew of pat answers or otherwise demonstrate a lack of sensitivity to the work of God, we miss the opportunity to serve Christ and the friend. If, on the other hand, a person has a good relationship with at least one gentle, wise Christian, the awakening gives opportunity for deeply important and significant conversations. If we pay attention, we can join the Holy Spirit's work by providing a listening ear and an open heart. We need not have all the right answers, but we do need to attend to the significance and potential transformation for one in such moments.

In standard theological terms, an awakened person eventually demonstrates a truly penitent attitude. "Penitence" means much more than remorse for moral misdeeds. It signals one's *readiness for the kind of change only God can produce.* Penitence[12] is dispositional, revealing a

---

11. James Loder in his work also offers a view of awakening that follows what he calls a classical model (by which he means practices that medieval Christian mystics developed to great effect). For a description of awakening according to Loder, see *Logic of the Spirit*, 65–66.

12. An earlier generation of church leaders distinguished two kinds of repentance: "judicial" and "evangelical." Judicial repentance refers to the deep sense of remorse that

new openness to respond to God's call. Thus, we have a second threshold moment, indicated by the new box below.

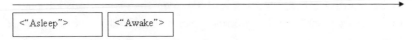

THE THRESHOLD: CONVERSION/FAITH/NEW BIRTH

All that has gone before us in this discussion lays the foundation for the next (and most crucial) threshold moment, which can go by several terms. Let me remind the reader again not to think of these terms as dictating a particular kind of experience. I do not think that a believer has to be able to assign a date and time for the moment of conversion, although I think it is wonderful that many people can. Of fundamental importance is that one can confidently give witness to living faith, to the reality of a *present* personal relationship with God in Christ; that one *knows* (is strongly confident) that one now is forgiven and restored to relationship with God and is presently walking, by the power of the Holy Spirit, in the way of Christ.

Taking care, therefore, not to set unnecessary limits for describing this threshold moment, we define Christian conversion as *consciously stepping into a new relationship with God*—Father, Son, and Holy Spirit. One image that always comes to my mind as I think about this moment is admittedly corny and old-fashioned. In scenes from the old romantic film comedies of the 1940s and '50s, we see the newly married bride and groom standing on the porch of their new home. As the camera moves in for the close-up, they look lovingly into each other's eyes; the groom scoops up his new bride into his arms, and carries her over the threshold into their home. That step over the threshold symbolizes the new union, this new beginning of life together. And, of course, it implies a "happily ever after."

---

people feel about their spiritual conditions and their accountability to God (or, perhaps, to a higher power of some sort short of their recognizing a personal God). Judicial repentance is most often accompanied by a desire to change or to "reform." Discovering that one lacks the power to bring about this reform can lead to discouragement, but it also can lead to evangelical repentance: the readiness to admit one's utter powerlessness to change, and thus to yield to God's transforming power and to accept God's grace in Christ. It would be helpful, I believe, to renew our use of such terms to help people describe their sense of their own spiritual conditions.

I think this picture serves as a useful analogy of the threshold experience that combines justification by faith and the new birth. John Wesley and numerous other Christian leaders[13] over the generations have spent much effort describing this moment. Wesley analyzed it according to two basic changes that take place. One is positional and relational (justification)—the change in relationship between God and human that effects a new status before God. The other part focuses on the change in our nature, or, to use the philosophical word, ontology.[14] The Bible describes the ontological changes as being "born of the Spirit" or "born from above" (see John 3). The new birth involves the transformation of the fundamental orientation (the "bent") of our desires and attitudes. Even though it may be hard (even impossible) to identify the precise threshold moment, still we can attest to the present reality of a living relationship with Christ, with the resultant change in our hearts. Christ the bridegroom,[15] through his Spirit, picks us up (notice the sheer giftedness of his work on our behalf) and carries us into the new relationship. Once we were largely unaware of the work of God in our lives. Now we have become not only aware, but readily say "yes" to that relationship with Christ. We are now attentive and hungry, yielding to and following our Lord.

The New Testament is replete with stories of this sort of change. On the Day of Pentecost in Acts 2, following Peter's sermon, many of the listeners were "cut to the heart," the Scripture says, and they asked, "What should we do?" The logic and tone of this passage indicates in short order an awakening to the compelling truth of the Gospel to which the apostles were giving witness. The hearers' question about what to do indicates a willingness to change ("repentance"), a desire to enter into a different

13. A name not well known outside of scholarly circles anymore is that of Philipp Spener, the German Lutheran pastor who became the leader of a movement known as Pietism. This movement had significant impact on the Evangelical Revival in Europe and America. Spener had dozens of published sermons on the new birth. For a good biography of Spener, see Stein, *Philipp Jakob Spener*.

14. "Ontological" derives from two Greek terms: *ontos* (being) and *logos* (study of). Ontology in philosophy and theology has to do with the study of being. God is sometimes described as Being Itself, and we are beings who derive their being from God as the ultimate Being.

15. I realize that I'm individualizing a concept that has more to do with the whole church. Christ is the bridegroom and the church is the bride, not just individuals. At the same time, in the broad catholic tradition of the church, certain authors have written of the experience in this individualized way. I think it is legitimate to do so as long as we keep the communal vision in mind as well.

kind of relationship with God. Peter counsels them that they will receive "forgiveness for [their] sins" upon repentance and trust (Acts 2:38). We could refer to other such biblical threshold moments: the Ethiopian eunuch; Saul on the road to Damascus; the Philippian jailer.

Admittedly, these accounts refer to pretty dramatic occasions, in part because biblical writers feel free to compress events in order to focus on the salient parts of the experience. Our threshold moments need not be so vivid. Again, I am not concerned about how one crosses the threshold. I am concerned *that* people are confident they have crossed it and have entered into a conscious journey of discipleship with Jesus Christ the Lord.

I have just described the relational change that we associate with justification by faith. Necessarily accompanying the relational change is the other (ontological) change, the beginning of transformation of one's being. As we noted above, the imagery of the new birth provides us the most vivid biblical metaphor. It is hard to use this word without conjuring up images that I wish to avoid, of high-pressure, manipulative invitations.[16] Many Christians cannot exactly tell you when they were born again. Analogous to the series of small threshold moments, the new birth can take place piecemeal through a series of mini-conversions. Nonetheless, with both the threshold moment and the real change wrought by the Holy Spirit in the new birth, at some point we recognize—even if we cannot identify it chronologically—a "moment" when the work of God is actualized in us in its justifying and transforming capacity.

The important question then becomes: how do we identify such a change? It seems simplistic to say, but it is true: we *feel* it.[17] "Feeling it" does not inevitably mean high emotion, but it does mean an adequate degree of conscious awareness coupled with emotionally tonal thoughts. I use "emotionally tonal" to describe these thoughts with reference to what

16. I am not criticizing evangelistic invitations or altar calls. I am criticizing high-pressure, emotionally manipulative tactics.

17. Some readers may be aware of the scholarly trajectory linking John Wesley's thought on the question of feeling and consciousness with the modern tradition of theological liberalism associated with Friederich Schleiermacher. Because this issue is complex, I cannot engage it here, but I do want to say that, given my cognitive view of emotions, I do not believe my description lapses into the "problem of romanticism" that some might think it does. This argument has to do with the priority in human nature of reason or the will. Forcing a choice of one over the other is a fool's errand leading to innumerable theological problems.

we saw in chapter 2. The point is that we almost never feel precisely nothing. We may be concentrating on some other aspect of a moment than our emotions, but emotions accompany thoughts. In other words, this change affects all the dimensions of the heart.

The change associated with the new birth comes first in terms of a fundamental reordering of one's *desires*. One now desires to know and to serve God and that desire seems to stick even if it ebbs and flows. The general thrust of one's life seems reverse of the case when one was asleep; no longer primarily self-interested, but God-interested. Whereas a person may have had moments of spiritual fervor and interest surrounded by long periods of "sleepiness," *now* the attitude reverses and the basic heart disposition leans toward interest in the things of God. Moments of spiritual lethargy and sin continue to occur, but the fundamental orientation has changed.

Just as God's Spirit was at work in the asleep and awakened person, now God's Spirit works in the threshold moment. In the threshold moment we can now talk about *justifying grace* and the beginning of *sanctifying grace*. At each point along the trajectory, it is the same Holy Spirit doing the work.

Let me digress briefly in order to deal with a problem that troubles many American Protestants. It has to do with our penchant for boiling down doctrine into manageable, communicable concepts. You have probably encountered what is often taken as the standard explanation for the significance and effect of Christ's death on the cross in the statement, "Jesus died for my sins." In dying, he *atones* for our sins. In some circles, if you can give a testimony that includes this statement, people will positively evaluate your experience and deem that you are legitimately a Christian.

In a bit more expanded form, you've probably read or heard something like this statement: Christ took our place on the cross. Christ's death on the cross pays the penalty for sin and satisfies God's wrath. Since Christ was without sin, his death alone atones. God the Father, seeing Christ's spotless life and substitutionary death, imputes Christ's righteousness to us. On this basis, through Christ's gift of his own life, God declares us righteous. The blood of Jesus covers our sin. This description sticks pretty closely to what theologians call the *judicial* or *forensic* view of atonement and focuses intently on our *status* relative to God. A version of this general view is also known as the substitutionary view of Christ's atonement.

While we are lawbreakers, this view of atonement does not do full justice to the nature and scope of human sin nor to the accomplishment of Christ's death. Sin also has a power, going far beyond our mere rebellion. Sin is like a Pandora's box; once we open the box, we are powerless to reverse the damaging effects. Paul's description of sin in Rom 7 is so helpful: "So I find it to be a law that when I want to do what is good, evil lies close at hand. For I delight in the law of God in my inmost self, but I see in my members another law at war with the law of my mind, making me captive to the law of sin" (7:21–23). Sin points not only to moral/legal transgression that negatively affects our status with God. Sin is also *power*, the power of death. Sin kills.

We are both perpetrators and victims of sin. And if somebody doesn't do something to rescue us, sin will destroy us all. But Christ has done exactly what we need. He not only pays the *penalty* of sin, he frees us from the *power* of sin. Here's a picture worth pondering: Christ conquered death by dying and rising from the dead! Therefore, in addition to the judicial aspects of Christ's atoning work, we need to see its liberative impact. God is not only a Righteous Judge. God is also our Strong Deliverer.

Another aspect of the atonement comes especially from the Eastern part of early Christianity. It describes sin as a disease, very much like a terminal illness.[18] This angle of vision helpfully illustrates the inborn (un-chosen) nature of sin, which, added to the view of sin as rebellion against a just God, helps us understand more fully Christ's work. People do not willingly choose to have a disease but we get sick nonetheless. In one sense, we don't choose to sin, yet we sin nonetheless. The power of sin exceeds choice. And we cannot heal ourselves. We desperately need a Physician. Christ the Physician has come to heal. The cross and resurrection demonstrate God's power over the disease of sin.

Thinking back to the initial "Jesus died for my sins" summary, we can thus begin to see how the popular tendency to lean exclusively on the description of one manageable and communicable aspect of the Gospel nevertheless leads to an impoverished view of what God is actually accomplishing in our lives. If we think of ourselves as "guilty sinners" only, then forgiveness and change in status is all that is required. But if we

18. I am not suggesting that someone who is ill is guilty of sin, yet, if we take the Scriptures seriously, we must admit that sometimes illness is the result of sin. This is a matter of careful pastoral wisdom.

look at the deeper impact of sin in our being (ontology), then we can see the need for more transformation than change in relationship. We need transformation of our very being.

We therefore once again can see how important it is to keep in view the expanded, more adequate view of "heart" that the Bible offers. For a more holistic view of what God accomplishes in Christ, we need to include substantial theological content to our common descriptions. Taking the time to ponder about and reflect on these ideas contributes to a change in the emotional tonality of our lives. The salient features of core theological ideas, when reflected upon prayerfully and openly, evoke comparable feelings (emotionally tonal thoughts) that begin to link with and shape our actual desires. This irreducible core of mental activities leads to real behavior changes in our lives, all under the guiding influence of the Holy Spirit.

These ideas about Christ's atoning work connect predominantly with the threshold moment of faith/new birth, even though, with the new birth, we begin to talk about the work of the Spirit in sanctification (making us holy). Thus, the notion of healing carries into discussions of the Christian life. So, to follow, we have in the threshold moment the work of the Spirit in *justifying grace* and we also have the evidence of the beginning of *sanctifying grace*.

In adding these terms to your vocabulary, I want to take care again to emphasize one thing: it is *all* the work of one and the same Holy Spirit. We are simply talking about the guiding, shaping activity of God—grace. So, our trajectory now looks like this:

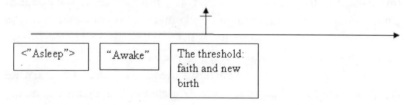

This moment (or series of moments) links justification with sanctification. Sanctification can be variously described, but commonly it refers to a similar two-part way of thinking: (1) being set apart for service to God (which parallels the relationship/positional aspect of justification) and (2) being made holy through the work of the Spirit, being renewed according to the image of God (which corresponds to the ontological or internal change or change in being). When we think of growth toward spiritual maturity, we are talking about sanctification.

Needing More Attention: Growth to/toward Maturity

We now come into full view of the main point of this book—spiritual maturity. The new birth/justification threshold marks the beginning of growth toward this goal. From this moment forward God calls us to grow in every aspect of life into the character of Christ, according to Scriptures like Eph 4:15: "But speaking the truth in love, we must grow up in every way into him who is the head, into Christ." We therefore need to have a good vision of what maturity looks like (it looks like Jesus) as well as an openness to seek and strive for it. We also need a plan for growing in this direction.

Getting that vision is somewhat tricky, because we are trying to avoid perfectionism (actually a form of self-righteousness) while not settling for less than the biblical vision of maturity. The popular antidote to perfectionism comes to us in the form of a bumper sticker that has been around for a long time: "Christians aren't perfect, just forgiven." Again we see how good biblical ideas do not fit very well in the small space of a bumper sticker. Although it is true that we are not flawless and that we are indeed forgiven, I have heard this statement used to excuse sinful behavior on the part of Christians. It is as if we are saying, "Hey, don't expect too much of us." The use of the bumper sticker therefore actually becomes a cover for sin by the very people who give witness to Jesus' dying to redeem them from sin!

John Wesley dealt with the same challenge. He called it "antinominanism," the belief that, because Jesus has done all that is necessary to save us, we need do nothing except believe in him. This careless attitude, Wesley was convinced, cut the very heart out of the Christian faith and gave followers of Jesus a standard trump card excuse for sin remaining in them. It is why he often referred to growing to maturity as having the mind of Christ *and walking* (lifestyle, behavior) as Christ walked. Couple this notion with others, like the promise that we are being renewed according to the likeness of God (Eph 4:24). And go a step further: if the Spirit of God is renewing God's image in us, then the supreme character of our lives is a love that looks like Jesus. Not only is Jesus our Savior; he is our Lord and Pattern. He is the Exemplar, par excellence, of Spirit-filled living. There is no excuse for antinomian bumper-sticker theology.

Subsequent chapters will add important elements to our description of spiritual maturity, but we can see here that we have actually already started a list that will help us evaluate ourselves. A Christian who is growing toward maturity consistently exhibits the following qualities:

- Experiences a persistent, constantly renewed set of desires that focus on knowing God and doing God's will

- Knows and feels a living faith in Christ, understanding that this faith is given on the basis of Christ's atoning work

- Is hungry to grow in knowledge of the things of God

- Demonstrates a humble, teachable *attitude*

- Grows in self-awareness and self-understanding, which is a form of penitence, the awareness of constant need for growth and change in God's grace

- Is willing to be held accountable for the highest of standards of the Gospel

- Feels love for God and recognizes the implications of Christ's call to love others through acts of service

- Seeks to make attitudes and behaviors consistent with the Pattern of Christ in all thoughts, words, attitudes, and actions, both in ethical behavior and in missional service

- In order to grow in all these ways, regularly engages in practices like worship, study, small group ministries, and service to others

This list shows how we might begin to recognize whether or not we are growing toward maturity. The problem with lists is that it tempts us to divide up that which cannot be divided. ("If I do 80 percent of the list, can I feel good about myself?") Therefore, notice the integrative vision, the whole self (heart), necessary for an adequate vision of spiritual maturity. We must pay attention to desires—the deeper ones as well as the surface level ones—which requires a growing degree of self-awareness and understanding. We need to know how ideas we have picked up from our faith context, our families and the larger society, shape our emotions, not just our thoughts. We need to have a sense of what motivates us to carry out Christian disciplines and other practices, including serving others. It's all of a package. And our little diagram now looks like this:

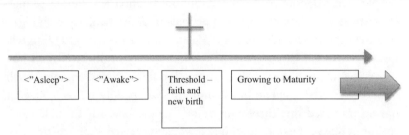

Can we actually believe that such a vision for maturity reflects the *normal* Christian life? I emphasize *normal* because we American Christians have a highly developed skill of picking and choosing the parts of the Christian life we like and are willing to entertain, while the tougher parts we let go. Thus the "normal" (as in, according to the norm) has been reduced to something that looks more or less like being a nice, morally upright person who is a regular church member. A different, more challenging view of the normal Christian life kicks into motion our fears about measuring up and our worry about slipping into perfectionism. We're good at avoiding the stuff that makes us feel bad. But if the Scriptures say that these attitudes refer to the normal Christian life, then we must pay attention. How are we doing?

For these reasons, we need to pay more attention to the sanctifying work of the Spirit on our dispositions. As I have already mentioned, Wesley talked about "holy tempers" and we have been using the term *dispositions* as a more modern synonym. Remember, dispositions have to do with tendencies to act. Dispositions exhibit emotional tonality while not reducing to mere feelings. If we want to grow toward maturity—remembering that growing to maturity is not optional—we must develop a keen awareness for what is going on in those dispositions. Part of the training we need for Christian maturity, therefore, is to learn how to interpret and read our own hearts, to gain in self-understanding without slipping into self-absorption. Sharpening this skill shows the necessity of community to help us. We will always be subject to blind spots.

FITTING THE TRAJECTORY TO COMMON MARKERS

Even though I have tried to make clear that individual experiences can and do vary dramatically, I am still concerned that the visual aid of the trajectory might unnecessarily restrict the way people understand and apply it. It might be helpful, therefore, to look at two standard ways that people across denominational and cultural boundaries attempt to mark the critical transition moments in people's faith, particularly with regard to the central threshold moment, in which we step consciously into rela-tionship with Christ and enter upon the journey of discipleship. I have called this moment variously "justification by faith and the new birth" and "conversion." The two most common ways people are recognized as having traversed this threshold are (1) "going forward" to make some sort of public profession of faith at a worship service, evangelistic meet-ing or rally or summer camp experience, and (2) the rite of confirmation, in more so-called mainline, liturgical denominational churches. Even though these two practices appear to be quite different from one another, those differences turn out to be fairly superficial. Let's try to unpack them a little and see how they connect to the trajectory toward maturity.

Many of us can tell stories about going to an evangelistic meeting or youth rally and finding ourselves going forward to the kneeling rail of a church, or to pray with a counselor at the end of a service. This method is so well known and has been used so widely that it can almost seem that we are not preaching the Gospel and leading people to Christ unless we use this form of proclamation evangelism. It comes with a great legacy, stemming from innovations developed by American revivalists, such as Charles Finney in the nineteenth century. The history of American Protestant Christianity is replete with dramatic stories and larger-than-life personalities like Finney or D. L. Moody or Billy Sunday or Aimee Semple McPherson. Of course, Billy Graham is the evangelist par excel-lence in relation to this practice.

In much of American Protestantism, therefore, revival meetings have been very prominent. They can be distinguished from the usual Sunday worship by a particular aim: the hymn singing, the special music, and the preaching all aim at conversion, and conversion is thought of as a crisis moment of decision. To use the more or less standard language associated with this approach, hearers ripe for the Gospel are put under conviction by the Holy Spirit in the course of a service—particularly by means of the preaching—and are led to a moment of decision, in which they accept Christ and feel God's forgiveness applied to their hearts.

In reading conversion narratives, while we may focus on the ac-tual moment of conversion, we can also get a sense of the Holy Spirit's

significant preparatory work in experiences prior to the moment of decision. Still, with regard to the revival approach, the witnesses place the emphasis of their conversion most heavily on the actual moment of decision.
According to our diagram above, the threshold moment from no faith to
faith is clear and distinct and often accompanied by great emotion.

After the decision, follow up is deemed highly important to help
the new convert become established in the faith and grow in Christ into
a consistent Christian and member of the congregation or Christian
group.[19] Although most groups recognize the importance of follow up,
in the environment in which so much emphasis is placed on a decision,
that decision becomes paramount. The sequence of what God is doing
also stands out clearly: first, God justifies the sinner as he/she crosses the
threshold into personal faith in Christ, *then*, through follow-up activities supposedly undertaken by local churches, God begins the sanctifying
work as the evangelistic team passes off the new believer to a local church.

I have just described the standard evangelistic or revivalist approach
to the threshold moment of our trajectory. Now let's look at the way of
confirmation classes and ritual exercised in typically more liturgical or
denominational churches. Most of them have some form of educational
experience leading to what they call "confirmation." In this arrangement,
usually students who are early- to mid-adolescent age (from twelve to
sixteen years old) meet regularly with a pastor or designated church leader to learn the church's beliefs, history, and particular emphases. Some
churches refer to these classes as "catechism" and others simply call them
"confirmation." After a period of instruction, the potential confirmands
are given the opportunity to express their faith publicly in a formal ritual, in which they answer doctrinal and covenantal questions before the
congregation. This event takes place as part of the usual Sunday service.
Sometimes they receive Christian baptism in this service, but for those already baptized as infants or children, baptism is not part of confirmation.
Sponsors, godparents, mentors, and other important persons surround
and support the confirmands as they take their vows in this service.

---

19. One well-known way of talking about this process of growth is in three general
steps: (1) evangelize, (2) establish, and (3) equip. The second step is full of what people
would call Christian education or discipleship activities. The third step seeks to help
people find their gifts so that they can, in turn, engage in ministries that share the Gospel
and edify the Body of Christ.

Churches preferring the catechetical or confirmation approach have increasingly incorporated adult forms of confirmation or new membership classes. This somewhat recent development has come in response to the growing awareness that large numbers of people did not grow up in the Christian faith or had only nominal experiences. These classes help adults grapple with the central claims of the Christian faith so that they can understand and fully engage in the decision that they may have made naively earlier in life or that they are coming to make in the present time.

Some observations about how these two general descriptions relate to our trajectory are now in order. First, on the surface, it appears that the evangelistic/revivalistic and the confirmation/catechism approaches are significantly different, but, in fact, they are not. Those in the revivalistic traditions often say that they eschew the "formalism" of ritual or liturgy, believing that the Holy Spirit has more freedom to act in a less formally constructed service. Anyone who has helped plan such services or has spent time participating in them knows, however, that they almost all follow a similar formula and structure: upbeat, enthusiastic worship, special music provided by someone who is not the usual local "talent," an invited preacher known to have evangelistic gifts, and an invitation at the end of a usually very intense sermon to come forward and either initially trust in Christ or to revive a dormant faith. The liturgy is not printed and it doesn't involve the congregation in the ways liturgy usually does, but there's a liturgy nonetheless that "tells a story" just like more formal liturgy does.

People from more expressly liturgical traditions normally don't like the (what they consider) emotionally heavy-handed qualities of the revival. Confirmation, therefore, sits within a larger framework of church life. In the revival tradition, the decision for Christ at the altar leads to active membership in a faith community. What we might call Christian education (or discipleship) *follows* the decision to be a disciple. In a more liturgical tradition, confirmands are already most likely part of the congregation and perhaps have been involved in various kinds of education. Confirmation is a step—a critical one, to be sure—toward becoming fully Christian. Since confirmation happens normally within a regular Sunday worship service and since confirmands have been preparing for the day for a period of time, the emotions associated with confirmation tend to be muted by comparison to a revival service. But like the revival service, the confirmands are asked for a decision to step into a conscious relationship with Christ, following him as full members of the congregation. If taken seriously, this decision is no less important than the decision to trust Christ made in an evangelistic rally. The process of education or discipleship may fall in different places in the span of time before or after a decision. In both, then, there is decision and education and there can be lots of emotion or little, in both approaches.

Likewise, there can be formalism in both approaches. By "formalism" I mean going through the motions without engaging the heart. If you grew up in a revivalist tradition, you probably remember feeling "pressure" to go forward at some point because you knew it was expected of you. If you grew up in a liturgical tradition that employs confirmation, you knew that when you entered sixth grade (or seventh grade or eighth grade) it was expected that you would take the classes and be confirmed. There is a reason for this pattern. Christian educators across the theological spectrum recognize that, developmentally, adolescents in their early to mid-teens start asking important questions about who they are and what kind of order governs the universe they inhabit. So, in one church, a student is encouraged to give his/her life to Christ (ritualized in the going forward to the altar or responding to an evangelistic invitation), and in another church, a student is encouraged to enroll in the confirmation class. Of course, some churches accommodate both approaches and there are other variations on the themes. The point is that formalism can be a problem in any church, any group, any tradition.

In either case, we can see the importance of good relationships in which maturing Christians give evidence of the reality and power of their relationship with God. In the former case—the standard evangelistic rally or service—one of the most significant factors in a person's *readiness* for conversion has to do with important relationships before and after the experience of conversion. Especially in our day, someone who models humble, joyful, transparent, growing Christian faith *shows* a person what being a Christian is all about. In this the relationship is a means of prevenient grace. But also, after conversion, the convert needs the help, support, and guidance of authentic Christian friends.

The same holds true for traditional churches. One reason why people accuse the confirmation approach to conversion of formalism has to do with the lack of significant relationship the confirmands have with other people in the congregation. Christian Smith has shown that, in addition to having an active faith as a teenager along with religiously active parents, the third most significant reason young people persevere in faith into their adult years has to do with crucial, formative relationships with other adults who are not their parents.[20]

Looking back across the trajectory, we can start to imagine its usefulness for helping us discern the quality of our growth toward maturity. It works both individually and corporately. A person can take stock of his or her life and draw a conclusion about where he or she stands at this moment and then make plans regarding how to grow. One may realize that one has never crossed that threshold into living faith in Christ or one may see significant growth in faith.

A similar possibility resides for congregational maturity. If you work in a congregation, make a list of all the programs your church supports. What are the aims of those programs? As I have interacted with congregations using this trajectory, I find that most often most of the church's activities aim at already-committed church members. It is easy to offer a kind of smorgasbord of activities for well-established members, but what about people hungering to know Christ? And what about people hungering to go on to maturity? We should think about each of these categories of people and be more strategic in our programming. The trajectory can help us think about other groups and conditions of people, so that our ministries can shift to minister to people across the spectrum.

If you and I could sit and talk, I might ask you where you see yourself fitting on this trajectory. Probably most people reading this book are already consciously following Jesus and looking for help to deepen their walk. If that is the case for you, then you're in the "growing Christian" part of the trajectory. But maybe you are discovering that you are not confident that you've crossed the threshold into full faith in Christ. His grace beckons and enables you to come.

---

20. The author heard Smith make this statement in a lecture at the Conference on Emerging Adulthood, Princeton Theological Seminary, November 6, 2010.

4 Power for Growth
Grace

By "the grace of God" is sometimes to be understood that free love, that unmerited mercy, by which I, a sinner, through the merits of Christ am now reconciled to God. But in this place it rather means that power of God the Holy Ghost which "worketh in us both to will and to do of his good pleasure." As soon as ever the grace of God (in the former sense, his pardoning love) is manifested to our soul, the grace of God (in the latter sense, the power of his Spirit) takes place therein. And now we can perform, through God, what to [humanity] was impossible.[1]

Wesley was convinced that the Christian life did not have to remain a life of continual struggle. He believed that both Scripture and Christian tradition attested that God's loving grace can transform our lives to the point where our own love for God and others becomes a "natural" response. Christians can aspire to take on the disposition of Christ, and live out that disposition within the constraints of our human infirmities. To deny this possibility would be to deny the sufficiency of God's empowering grace—to make the power of sin greater than that of grace.[2]

1. Wesley, "The Witness of Our Own Spirit," in *The Works of John Wesley*, 1:309.
2. Maddox, *Responsible Grace*, 188.

GRACE SHRUNK TO FIT

If ever there were a misused, misunderstood word in popular Christian conversation, it is "grace." You surely have heard someone say (I've said it myself), "We need to err on the side of grace," meaning some sort of indulgence or benefit of the doubt, aimed at someone who has stumbled or made a mistake. Of course, we should be flexible and generous and merciful, but does this apply to the biblical description of grace? For example, when Paul says in Rom 5:20, "Where sin abounds, grace abounds all the more," what is he talking about? Does he mean this kind of indulgence that we so easily attach to "grace"?

Let me play out a common scenario among Christians today. If I am studying the Scripture and want to find the meaning of a biblical word, where do I go for resources, since I probably do not possess many (or any) books in my own library that deal with these questions? I go to what is most readily at hand for many people—the Internet—and do a Google word search. Probably toward the top of the returned hits will come the Wikipedia[3] article that seems to hit the target. In the entry for "divine grace" we find probably the currently most often referred-to Christian understanding of grace: "In Christianity, grace is 'unmerited favor' from God." Think of how many times you have heard reference to grace in terms of unmerited favor. In that Wikipedia article, there is a second part to the definition: "In theology, *grace* may be described as 'enabling power sufficient for progression.'"[4] You'll also find a block quote that combines these two thoughts, from a well-known theologian, J. I. Packer. It explains that grace is God's "love in action toward men who merited the opposite of love." The article continues by distinguishing "grace" and "mercy," and we get the classic description of grace as getting a benefit (salvation) we *do not* deserve and mercy as not receiving the punishment that we *do* deserve. In a matter of a few lines, we get what usually looks like the whole package of a standard, basic, biblical explanation.

So as not to jump prematurely to a conclusion, let's see if we can find another source to corroborate or qualify what we just learned from Wikipedia. "Theopedia" is another accessible online source, which identifies its content as biased toward "conservative evangelical" thinking, but actually this grace language is so common that people who would not

---

3. Many academics are highly critical of using Wikipedia. I am not one of them.

4. Online: http://en.wikipedia.org/wiki/Divine_grace.

identify as conservative evangelical most likely use it as well. Typing in "grace" or "grace of God," we get the following statement in the first line of the entry: "Grace is unmerited favor."[5] Ah, the exact same definition as Wikipedia! Reading down through the Theopedia article, I see the same connection between God's mercy and grace, just as I had done with the Wikipedia entry. If I were unaware of the doctrinal debates over grace throughout church history, I would reasonably conclude that grace unquestionably means, "unmerited favor," because I have now checked two sources and they say exactly the same thing. I add to my thinking my memory of what I have heard Bible teachers say, reinforcing the notion of grace as "getting what I don't deserve," and I have a well-established interpretive framework for God's grace.

When pastors, preaching from texts that mention grace or mercy, repeat the above descriptions, we seem to be learning "what the Bible teaches" and, in fact, all that the Bible teaches. We have what appears to be a good, solid definition, and that sense of clarity and firmness sufficiently settles the question in our minds. Subsequently, when we hear sermons on divine grace, we have already in place an established reference point and think that we know exactly what to think. But I want to argue that we don't really know, yet. We have only gotten a good start, and, if we want to be biblical Christians, we're going to need to dig some more and add to our understanding of grace.

Much of the work I have just summarized focuses mainly on *the means by which God offers salvation*. Hence the emphasis rightly falls on the atoning work of Christ, which reveals both God's grace and mercy. The penalty for sin falls on Christ, not on us. The gift of salvation is offered through the cross and resurrection of Christ, rather than on our efforts. In the way this line of thinking is normally developed, therefore, we wind up following the trajectory that leads us to a positional description of salvation: guilty sinners are forgiven and accepted into God's family by virtue of God's grace. And if you go back to the chapter on the trajectory of spiritual maturity, you will see that we called this moment (however people experience it) the threshold into a relationship with God. Justification focuses on the change in relationship, as well as the change in position or status relative to God's holy judgments. The description of grace offered above fits very well within this framework.

---

5. Online: http://www.theopedia.com/Grace.

But what about once a person has become a conscientious, born-again follower of Jesus? What about living the Christian life? What about sanctification? Now, return with me to that first Wikipedia article on grace and notice the second part of the description: "enabling power sufficient for progression." This part of the definition, inherently connected to our goal of spiritual maturity, seems almost completely lost to the present generation of Christians.

If you take the time to read the entire entry, you will find a fairly full description of various viewpoints on divine grace, representing parts of the Christian tradition from Calvinist (Reformed) to Wesleyan-Arminian to Orthodox. "Ah," we might conclude, "the rest of this article is about fine points of doctrine, therefore not important for the practicalities of daily life." The studious, doctrinally inclined person may take time to work it through, but, for most of us, "grace as unmerited favor" works just fine. It is pretty easy not to pay much attention to "grace as enabling power." Armed with this understanding, whenever we read "grace" in the Bible, we read onto it our background belief about grace and assume that we have a biblically adequate idea.

I argue that this common practice produces a number of serious problems tied explicitly to the practicalities of the Christian life that people disinterested in the fine points of doctrine think they can avoid. To illustrate my point, let's take a classic text on grace, Eph 2:8–9, in both the New Revised Standard and the New International Versions:

> (NRSV) For by grace you have been saved through faith, and this is not your own doing; it is the gift of God—not the result of works, so that no one may boast.

> (NIV) For it is by grace you have been saved, through faith—and this not from yourselves, it is the gift of God—not by works, so that no one can boast.

It seems perfectly acceptable to slip into the "grace-not-works" interpretation because 2:9 clearly says so. And because we tend to let verse numbers limit the way we see biblical passages, we might feel satisfied that we adequately understand this verse and move on to other verses that mention grace. If I follow the common explanation of Eph 2:8–9 and stick with the "grace-as-unmerited-favor" view, then I wind up with a claim that goes like this: "I am saved by grace. I do not have to do anything to earn my salvation." It would appear that we developed and confirmed an adequate concept of grace from both the Bible and our Wikipedia research.

I want to point out two common problems from this reading, neither of which easily appears to us in the push-and-pull of daily life. First, even though dedicated teachers provide important contextual information when explaining Scripture texts, we also try to make the key points in memorable ways such that people remember them. The unintended consequence is that people often remember basic definitions and lose track of the nuance that the context gives the point. Second, also with regard to biblical exposition, we often do not sufficiently recognize the impact of interpretive traditions. We can give the impression that this one way of interpreting a text is the only way that text can be interpreted, with no room for variation. Especially in the present case, with regard to teachings about divine grace, our emphasis on grace-not-works was forged in the fires of long-ago controversy.

We will return to the point about controversy in a moment. For now, let's return to Eph 2:8–9 and see what we might be missing if we go always to our default understanding of grace. If you read the whole passage, Eph 2:1–10, and notice the other topics that Paul connects to grace, you can start to see other very important points. First, the "you" in this passage (as in, "By grace, *you* have been saved") translates the second person plural, for which we do not have a separate English word any longer. "You" is both singular and plural for us. In other languages (like New Testament Greek) there is also a second person plural "you" that is a different word from the singular "you." Most of the time, because of our culture's individualist assumptions, we think that "you" means the singular, but in Eph 2, it does not. It means something like "you all." Thus, while realizing the necessity of personal (individual) appropriation of the Gospel through faith, we can also see that Paul's primary aim is not about making sure people know they don't have to earn their salvation. That concern stands out more clearly in Galatians, perhaps. Rather, he is emphasizing the utter "God-givenness" of this action and this action has particular implications for the whole world.

This claim leads to a second. Reading the whole of chapter 2, we see Paul proclaiming that, in Christ as the head over all things, a "new humanity" ("new man" in the New International Version and others[6]) is

6. The Greek term is *kainon anthropon*, which literally translates "new man," but in fact means "new humanity," because the context shows that Paul is talking about a cor-

being formed. This point has to do with God's sweeping involvement in history. In this case, Jewish and Gentile believers in Jesus—people who once were bitterly hostile toward one another—are becoming a new people in Christ. This marvelous work is all of God's grace. In their sin, those Ephesian believers (whether Jew or Gentile) had been dead. Now they have been made alive in Christ and have been formed into a new commonwealth. Gentiles are joint heirs and fellow citizens with Jews in God's great new economy in Christ.

The concept of grace, when reduced simplistically to the notion of "unmerited favor," interpreted through our individualistic assumptions in part and, in another part, read with the controversy between Protestants and Catholics over whether works help to merit salvation, simply does not do justice to what the Eph 2 text says. This reduced understanding leads to more than a conceptual error. *It stunts growth.* This minimized view keeps us locked in an individualized understanding of faith and salvation and focuses on *what we do not have to do* rather than on what God is doing through us. We need to pay attention to the very real prospect that we cannot arrive at maturity—the full measure of the stature of Christ (Eph 4:13)—either as individual Christians or as communities of believers if we wrap ourselves in superficially comforting, but unnecessarily limited, interpretations. Ideas matter.

I work with young people, most of them university students. I hear again and again this stripped-down, sound bite version of grace: "getting what I don't deserve" and "unmerited favor." It almost always comes in tandem with the related notion they express, that grace therefore means that we don't have to work for our salvation. It so easily degenerates into the notion that being a Christian means just believing in Jesus and nothing else of any import. I can tell you, many students on college campuses express quite sincerely that they are Christians because they can say that they know that Jesus died for their sins. They also know the "biblical" definition of grace that I've been criticizing, but nothing else in their lives gives any indication of the life-transforming impact of grace. Grace is set up against grace. Many students are missing how grace continues to operate *in them* even though they understand, at least in a basic sense, what God has done *for them.* But this attitude I find not only in college students. It's everywhere.

---

porate "new man."

HOW DID WE GET HERE?

When we read the Bible, we do so aided by a host of sources that, most of the time, remain hidden to our conscious thoughts. We have before us the cumulative effect of, in this case, centuries of teaching and controversy. To gain insight into why this truncated version of grace has become so dominant, I need to take you on a brief tour of the history of a doctrine.

Most Christians have at least heard references to and perhaps have even read something about the controversy between Martin Luther and the Roman Catholic Church in the 1500s, a controversy known commonly as the Protestant Reformation.[7] The fundamental "Protestant"[8] understanding of grace grew out of a combination of Luther's personal experience and his theological exploration in controversy with the Roman Catholic Church. Even though he was a priest and a highly trained theologian, for years he felt tortured by lack of confidence regarding his own standing with God. It all hinged on his understanding of the term "justice."[9] The official version of the Bible used then was the Latin Vulgate. In the book of Romans, the Greek term for righteousness, *dikaosune*, is translated into the Vulgate as *iustitia*, justice. *Iustitia*, read in the Middle Ages, was understood in terms of the administration of justice, notably in the way a monarch might hand out punishment for injustice.

We must pay attention, therefore, not only to Luther's experience, but also to the late Middle Ages European context. Powerful monarchs and emperors could dispense "justice" with a strong and sometimes violent hand. Even the Church, which in those days served as part of the government apparatus, had the Inquisition to sniff out and curtail heretical beliefs and it could do so in harshly coercive violent ways.[10] In Luther's day the term "justice" had a heavier, more ominous feel to it than it does today for people living in democratic societies.

7. It should not surprise you that Catholic historians do not typically call the Protestant Reformation a reformation. In recent years, historians on both sides of this issue have softened and modified their telling of this story.

8. The term "Protestant" came to be associated with those groups of Europeans who revolted against the doctrinal error, moral corruption, and abuse of power by the Roman Catholic pope and some of his underlings.

9. A classic, elegantly readable biography of Martin Luther is Bainton's *Here I Stand*. Google it. It's worth the read. Bainton does a very good job of showing Luther's spiritual struggle.

10. Popular notions about the Inquisition are often distorted by anti-Catholic biases.

Partially influenced by this contextualized sense of "justice," for a long time Luther understood God's justice as divine wrath, God's anger over sin. "Justice" had mostly to do with God's "right" to punish sinners. And Luther knew himself to be a vile sinner, even though he was a priest and living in a community of monks completely devoted to prayer, study, and worship. He thought of himself this way because he knew the gap between his outward behavior and his inner feelings, thoughts, and impulses. Even though Luther rigorously followed the disciplines of his community and knew that, especially as a religious leader he was supposed to love God, he admitted that he actually hated God because of this sense of God's justice as wrath. And hating God is a damnable sin. He was trapped. The harder he worked, the more ineffectual he felt, because he simply could not conquer every inward sin.

Then came Luther's "tower experience,"[11] his moment of illumination in which he saw that God's righteousness is actually made manifest in God's mercy, through the cross of Jesus Christ. This new insight completely revolutionized his thinking and his experience (notice how the two go together). Leading up to this point, Luther had been studying both Rom 1:17 and Hab 2:4, which say, "The righteous/just shall live by faith." In faith, the guilty sinner throws herself or himself on the mercy of God, and God, who is rich in mercy, accepts the sinner without any meritorious works from the human side of things. This action on God's part happens on the basis of Christ's all-sufficient atoning work. God's justice (wrath) is carried out in Christ on our behalf and we guilty sinners go free by trusting in Christ. That we find the ability to throw ourselves on God's mercy, that we exhibit this attitude of faith, is itself purely a gift of God—God's grace.

With this newfound understanding of the basis of the Christian life—faith as an expression of God's gift of grace—Luther set out to correct the abuses of a medieval ecclesial system held hostage by Renaissance popes and corrupt leaders. For years, even long before his new evangelical understanding of grace, he agonized over the moral decay of the clergy. In

11. Whether or not it actually happened in the way historians have told the story is a matter of dispute, but for our purposes we can confidently say that Luther had a moment of insight (divine illumination?). The euphemism "tower experience" refers to the suggestion that Luther was actually going to the bathroom when he had his great moment of insight. In the late medieval period in which Luther lived, the toilet was in the tower of a castle. The toilet waste actually was channeled through a chute that would take the waste outside into a nearby stream.

1510, for example, he had made a pilgrimage to Rome and had discovered a shocking degree of decadence and lack of concern by clergy—by the very people appointed to administer the means of grace to the faithful— for the holy things of God. He saw this decay literally in the seat of power for the Catholic Church. In 1517, armed with this new freedom and joy in Christ, he began to criticize the Church's excesses and errors. Many people have heard of the 95 Theses, a list of statements that Luther posted publicly for the purpose of open debate.

One of the foundational points of conflict had precisely to do with the means by which we are saved: is it grace alone or is it a combination of grace and human works? Luther came down on the side of grace alone (*sola gratia*). Luther tended to separate the acts of "justification" and "sanc-tification." "Justification" is what God did in Christ on the cross and can be received in a moment as we place our trust in Christ. "Sanctification" is the process of growth that follows justification and can be distinguished from it. Standard teaching in the Roman Catholic Church, in that day, tended to overlay justification and sanctification, so that both processes took all of one's life to appropriate. One received both justification and sanctification by availing oneself of the Church's sacraments. In practical terms, this approach seemed to place the burden of efficacy on human ef-fort, which looked a lot like the attempt to merit salvation. "Faith," in this system, meant assenting to what the Church taught and doing what the Church required. As a consequence, "grace" meant participating in the Church's sacraments. For Luther, as I pointed out above, "faith" had come to mean a radical trust in Christ's cross and "grace" was God's profound favor given without merit through Christ.

This view of grace and faith inherited from the Protestant Reformation is deeply formative of anyone in the Protestant tradition, whether one belongs to a "mainline" church or an independent Bible church. Luther's theological concerns, and the tradition of interpretation that developed from them, shed true light on the Christian faith. But we also need to keep in mind that circumstances vary from one period to another, which gives doctrines nuance and shades of meaning that need our attention. Our controversies today are nothing like what Luther faced.

The second major circumstance that shapes our understanding took place in the United States and lands us within another kind of controversy within the church. Much of today's divisions and wariness among "con-servative evangelical" and "liberal" or "moderate" Christians hearkens back to ideas forged in the conflicts between Protestants. They are most commonly known in church history as Fundamentalists and Modernists, terms needing some description.

In nineteenth-century America, a broad Protestant evangelicalism dominated society. This period saw the growth of so-called mainline churches like the Methodism of which I am a member. As denominations grew, the need for trained clergy also grew and biblical institutes (usually now called seminaries) began to proliferate. In order to have qualified professors for these schools, many of the most promising candidates went to Europe to study theology and biblical studies, most often in Germany, where many famous professors were doing groundbreaking, cutting-edge scholarship. The American PhD students-become-professors, upon returning to their teaching posts, brought the new scholarship and began to train American pastors. This (largely German) source for new theological and biblical ideas, coupled with the surge of influence of the scientific method, began to put strong pressure on traditional Christian beliefs about how God works in the world (only through natural means alone or also through identifiable supernatural acts?), about the nature and work of Jesus (divine and human or really only human with a heightened God-consciousness?), and about the nature and authority of the Bible. All these concerns have direct bearing on how people understand and live the Christian life. This new way of thinking was called "Modernism" or "Liberalism."

The Modernists were generally committed to reading the Bible as a set of historically formed documents, even if they continued to uphold some understanding that the Scriptures (or the Scriptures' authors) were divinely inspired. Reading the Bible historically went along with trying (in the discipline of theology) to get as close as possible to what the earliest followers of Jesus actually thought about him, and, even more importantly, how Jesus himself understood his identity and mission. The "historical Jesus," and the true one, these scholars thought, was buried under centuries of philosophical and theological add-ons that contribute to hiding the faith that Jesus preached. From their perspective, then, being a biblical Christian meant getting at the "real Jesus" that the first-century disciples would have known. Given these scholars' penchant for modern scientific assumptions, the historical Jesus generally meant a powerful, but non-supernatural Jesus. The agenda of the historical Jesus was ethical—the Kingdom of God. He did not really claim to be Messiah,

Christ and Son of God. The later church claimed this belief, but not Jesus himself. Being a biblical Christian, then, according to Modernism, boiled down essentially to following Jesus' teachings, such as are summarized in the Sermon on the Mount, rather than trusting in the blood of Christ to atone for our sins.

Finally, Modernism followed the developing theories about education that were coming to the fore at the same time. These forces acted upon and reinforced each other. In mainline churches (at least in the more middle-class urban churches), they began to downplay revivalism and instantaneous conversion. In their place they put Christian education and development of beliefs and practices by natural means. "Grace," in this modernist way of looking at things, tended to follow a natural trajectory of human growth and development, rather than calling for a supernatural infusion. If you think through the various aspects of Christian doctrine regarding sin, the work of Christ and the Christian life, you can begin to see some of the implications of this new way of thinking.

To the group of people eventually known as "Fundamentalists," the Modernists appeared to give up wholesale the core doctrines of Christianity, changing the very foundations of the faith into something quite alien to the "faith once delivered."[12] In large part, the Fundamentalists emphasized virtually the opposite of what the Modernists were saying. They upheld varying expressions of the authority and reliability of Holy Scripture as divinely revealed, rather than historically formed.[13] Early Fundamentalist scholars held to a propositional view of divine truth, meaning that biblical truth could be fully and adequately captured in propositions—literal statements understandable by all. In other words, although these Fundamentalist teachers knew that the Bible was filled with metaphors and stories (that is, took a narrative form), with regard to the doctrines that Christians need to hold to the faith, those doctrines could be stated propositionally.

---

12. *Fundamentalist* is a bad word these days. It implies narrowness, rigidity, ignorance, and violence. But a fundamentalist of the sort I am describing would not fit that description. Historically, the term comes from a series of pamphlets, called "The Fundamentals," that were published as occasional papers and then were collected into a two-volume work. See Torrey, *The Fundamentals*.

13. Here, words like *inerrancy* and *infallibility* come to mind, with regard to the nature and authority of the Bible.

Fundamentalists thus proclaimed Jesus' virgin birth, his miraculous works, his miraculous works, his atoning sacrifice as the Substitute for sinful humanity, his bodily resurrection on Easter morning, and his literal, personal return to earth in glory and power. In his death he satisfied the demands of justice from a holy God. In taking our place on the cross, Jesus exacted justice on sin, by which a just God extended mercy to undeserving sinners. Fundamentalists became known as Evangelicals by the late 1940s and it is a term still used today.[14]

Perhaps you know this story of Protestantism's American division. The point here is that this narrative continues to exercise powerful influence in the way we read the Scriptures, therefore also in the way we think about grace. Whether using the term or not, people who fit the Modernist stream tend to think of grace in more natural terms. To put it in a rather bland and unfair way, God works (usually) quietly through the natural, normal processes of life, though God can, whenever working for justice, show up in dramatic (but not necessarily miraculous) fashion through prophetic advocacy. Grace for Modernists (better known as Progressives today) does not connect so closely to the atoning work of Christ, for reasons already mentioned.

On the other hand, the standard evangelical definition of grace continues to emphasize unmerited favor offered to sinners through the cross and resurrection of Christ. For a long time evangelicals have thought of themselves as maintaining a biblical view of core Christian doctrines. It helps us understand why certain aspects of grace have been emphasized to the virtual exclusion of others within evangelical circles. Against that older controversy from the Protestant Reformation, we uphold grace and faith over against human effort as a way of meriting salvation. Against the new Modernism or Progressivism, we uphold a strong view of biblical authority and the supernatural work of grace revealed in Christ's death and resurrection.

Many mainline Protestants fully subscribe to the evangelical understanding of the doctrines mentioned above, particularly with regard to grace. As a member of a mainline denomination, I am one of them. I have nonetheless begun to worry about the unintended consequences associated with ways in which evangelicals uphold these doctrines. In terms of practice and experience, as we look back over the summary of this

14. Every term has problems, and this case is no different. I leave aside a number of useful qualifications for the sake of clarity and brevity.

chapter, we see that what has become a common view of grace among today's rank-and-file believers so emphasizes the positional impact of Christ's atonement that we have almost completely lost the vision for the transformation of character that goes with the change in status. This, too, is a work of grace every bit as much as the change in relationship with God effected through Christ and appropriated by faith. In other words, we are not paying enough attention to grace as the sanctifying work of the Holy Spirit. In popular Christian culture we see the stripped-down grace. Grace is a gift. We don't earn it. We don't have to work for it. It brings us blessings and benefits, including heaven. But it doesn't seem to do much *in us now* that makes us resemble the Lord whom we say we serve. It does not *fit us* for Kingdom work, for embodying Christ's mission.

I've taken a long time to get to the constructive part of this chapter, but I think it is very important for the reader to have some of this background in order to make progress in the Christian life. In making the critique that I have made, I want to emphasize again that I have no intention of *tearing down* one idea of grace and *replacing* it with another. I do, on the other hand, want to *add to* this well-known understanding of grace. In addition to what Christ has done *for* us, let us look at what Christ—through the Spirit—does *in* us. I want to answer the question, Where is the *power* for faithful Christian discipleship? It resides in the same concept: grace.

GRACE AS THE POWER OF THE SPIRIT

The basic Greek term in the New Testament for grace is *charis*—gift. However, it is a very supple word. To cover the various meanings and ways it is used in the New Testament takes up a little more than two pages (of very small print) in a standard Greek Lexicon.[15] In addition to the well-known sense of divine favor, grace includes ideas like goodwill and thanksgiving. If you belong to a sacramental church, Holy Communion is referred to as Eucharist, which means giving thanks. Notice *charis* in the word *Eucharist. Charisma* is another word that we recognize. A person has "charisma." People argue about "charismatic" gifts. In these cases we can think of features or characteristics of a person that stand out as giving that person some kind of influence or even power.

---

15. A lexicon is like a dictionary.

As we get into the meat of a study on grace, we will encounter forms of this word *charis*. We will follow a pattern similar to what we did in chapter 1, where we studied the Bible's description of maturity as *teleios*, arriving at the goal or achieving the aim (of God). We will likewise briefly examine a range of uses of the word *grace* from the New Testament. Because the term appears so frequently, we cannot do an extensive study, but I think even this surface review will demonstrate the need to see grace as power to live according to Christ's nature and will. Grace in this sanctifying sense is the power of the Holy Spirit at work in individuals and communities to embody the character and ministry of Jesus. Grace is God's enabling power to grow to maturity.

Grace in the Book of Acts

In the book of Acts, some form of the Greek word for "grace" is used seventeen times. At least six of these occasions clearly show a connection between grace and some visible effect among the people. In other words, the references indicate that because of grace, Christians show a Christ-like quality to the Christian life visible to others. In Acts 4:33, for example, grace and power are linked. The apostles testify to the resurrection of the Lord and the believers gathered in Jerusalem show God's grace by their generosity. In Acts 6:8, Stephen, martyred eventually for his faith, does signs and wonders "full of grace and power." Barnabas, delegated by the church in Jerusalem to check on the new Christians at Antioch, "saw the grace of God" in them and rejoiced (11:23). What grace did he see? Of course, the very fact of the existence of believers among the Gentiles in Antioch is a sign of God's grace, but it goes beyond the bare fact to the kind of community they were becoming. In Iconium, Paul and Barnabas speak the word of God with boldness, in spite of persecution and violence against them. God demonstrated grace "by the signs and wonders" done through them (14:3).

It seems clear, therefore, that, in Acts "grace" links with some visible effect and, in certain cases, explicitly manifests divine power (signs and wonders) among and within believers in Jesus. That people ought to be able to see the grace of God in human lives should give us pause and, as I asked above, prompt us to examine the cause of this visible effect. For these reasons, we can see why understanding the Spirit's sanctifying activity is crucial to spiritual growth.

Thinking of God's grace as God's gracious activity in our lives prompts questions. I use the first person pronoun here purposefully. I hope you, as you read, will ask them personally as well.

1. What is God doing *now* in my life? In what way can I and others *see* that work?

2. What is the connection between God's work *in me* and God's expectation (purpose) *for me*? And perhaps more distantly:

3. What is God doing in the Christian community of which I am part? What does God expect of *us* and how is God's grace working to aim us in that direction?

Asking these questions moves us away from simply regarding grace as a divine benefit so that we can enjoy a certain status with God or so that we can be confident in our place in heaven.

Grace in Romans and Galatians

Charis appears twenty-two times in the book of Romans and seven times in Galatians. I link these two books because of their similarity in concerns regarding grace and the law. In both books, Paul is keen to make clear that grace operates apart from the Mosaic Law. His main reason for emphasizing this point, is to show how and why Gentile believers in Jesus do not need first to convert to the Jewish faith in order to be welcomed into the people of God. Paul goes to some length, then, to demonstrate *historically*, that Abraham received God's grace prior to the Law (Rom 4; Gal 3). *Theologically*, he argues that the purpose of the law was to reveal (1) the futility of self-righteousness and (2) the blessedness of grace as an unmerited divine gift offered in Christ.

We find in Romans and Galatians some of the language that shapes what often is called the "judicial view" of salvation, to which I referred earlier. If you think in terms of law, then grace apart from the law frees one from the judgment of the law. It is logical and appropriate, therefore, that we have connected grace to these judicial or positional notions. On the basis of such biblical references, we think of ourselves as guilty sinners in need of God's grace. The relevant passages in Romans and Galatians lend support to this way of thinking about salvation. But there is more to the picture even in Romans and Galatians than this legal/judicial view.

Consider this question: once we are justified—that is, God has for-given us, declared us just, accepted us adopted children on the basis of Christ's atoning work—what then? Once people have crossed the thresh-old into discipleship, what does grace have to do with the Christian life besides keeping us in right relationship with God (which, of course, is hugely important)? Well, grace continues to work to sanctify us (make us holy) and to enable us to carry out the work that Christ intends his Body to undertake.

Even in Romans and Galatians we see examples of this sanctifying aspect of grace that help round out and fill in the notion of divine favor as God's purposeful activity in our lives through the work of the Spirit. It takes us beyond the notion of unmerited benefit to the idea of divine enablement. In Rom 12, for example, the Spirit enables us to live together in the Body of Christ and to minister in the power of Christ by means of the spiritual gifts. Keep in mind that the Greek word for "gift" and "grace" is the same. Rom 12 shows the grace-gift as a divine enablement. The Spirit works in our individual hearts and in our Christian communities. Notice the purpose of the presence of such gifts: Christians witness to the importance of a certain kind of community! We are to love without hypocrisy. We are to be gentle and humble. We are to serve the Lord with zeal, to be patient in suffering and persistent in prayer. These injunctions from Paul are as important for understanding grace as are his descrip-tions of grace over law.[16]

Likewise in Galatians: we have taken note of the emphasis on grace as the cause of justification, rather than (as the Judaizers argued) follow-ing the Law, beliefs and behaviors which negate the effect of the cross of Christ. Paul has made that point forcefully in the first four chapters of the book. We know these ideas well. But consider what he says in Gal 5:4–6 regarding grace: "You who want to be justified by the law have cut your-selves off from Christ; you have fallen from grace. For through the Spirit, by faith, we eagerly wait for the hope of righteousness. For in Christ Jesus neither circumcision nor uncircumcision counts for anything; the only thing that counts is *faith working through love* [emphasis added]." Paul has taken a step beyond explaining the relationship between grace and the law. He is now talking about the way the Galatians actually live their Christian discipleship. If grace is working in them, they will not only trust

16. The same could be said for 1 Cor 12 and 14, where we find lists of spiritual gifts.

Christ as Savior. They will show their faith through acts motivated by love. Faith works through attitudes and actions that demonstrate the love of Christ.[17]

We can see the specifics of faith working through love a few verses later, when Paul contrasts the deeds of the flesh with the fruit of the Spirit. Although we do not find the word *grace* used here, because of what Paul has been saying, we see the connection to what he has already asserted. "Grace" (divine activity) is made visible in the Galatians' lives by the fruit of the Spirit. And notice the fruit the Spirit produces: love, joy, peace, patience, kindness, generosity, gentleness, faithfulness, and self-control. The work of grace subsequent to what God has accomplished in the atoning work of Christ is to transform the believers so that their lives manifest these qualities. If we show the fruit of the Spirit, then we look like Jesus.

Ephesians and Philippians

Charis (grace) appears twelve times in the short book of Ephesians and three times in the even shorter Philippians. Regarding Ephesians, numerous scholars have noted how it distinctively portrays Christ as Lord of the entire cosmos.[18] His sovereign lordship encompasses all of human history, all governments, all principalities and powers. There is no public/private division, in which governments rule the world while Christ "rules" in individual human hearts. He rules, period. This conviction about God's cosmic plan or administration (the Greek work is *oikonomia,* from which comes our word "economy") provides a controlling concept for the entire book, an important point to keep in mind.

So, what is God doing in history through the lordship of the Son? By grace, he is forming a new people, a new humanity. In Ephesians 1, we notice "us" language and "you" language. Verses 3 through 12 use "us." Then, in verse 13, the text switches to "you" (second person plural) and carries on from there. Who is the "us" and who is the "you"? The "us" are the Jews, members of the covenant people of God who have trusted Jesus as Messiah. The "you" are the Gentiles who, in Christ, are now by grace added to the people of God.

17. See also Phil 2:5–8 for the same vision.

18. A good Bible dictionary on the book of Ephesians will explicate this point. For more detailed material, see Hoehner, *Ephesians,* or Lincoln, *Ephesians.*

Exactly how is grace operative in this vision, beyond the well-known truth that, though the Ephesians were dead in sin, they have been made alive in Christ? Grace also effects the formation of this new people of God, this "new humanity," formed from two groups formerly hostile to one another, Jew and Gentile. As people's relationship with God changes, so does their relationship with each other. Christ "is our peace," having torn down "the dividing wall of hostility." Yes, we find reference to his "abolishing" the law—which might tempt us to slip into that individualized law-grace opposition—but let's be careful to stick with how the passage frames this comment about the law. Abolishing the law is a step in forming the new humanity in Christ.

The city of Ephesus was prominent in Asia Minor (modern Turkey) for three major reasons, touching on three of the most important aspects of human existence: government, economics, and religion. Ephesus was a Roman provincial capital—the capital of Asia. Being a center for (Roman) government gave it a status unequaled in the region. It held the title, "First and Greatest Metropolis of Asia."[19] Likewise, Ephesus was a major commercial center, as a harbor city situated in the conjunction between the Cayster River and the Aegean Sea. Finally, it was home of one of the Seven Wonders of the World in that day—the temple to Artemis (Diana), making it a major religious center as well. If you lived in that region and wanted to go "where the action is," Ephesus would certainly be the place to go.

This backdrop provides the help we need in grasping the staggering impact of God's grace on a group of people who embody and witness to God's plan for all history. We will return to the context of Ephesus in chapter 6 when we look at the corporate dimension of spiritual maturity and simply say at this point that Ephesus was regionally prominent in a number of significant ways. It provides a highly significant backdrop to the place where God's power is revealed. In a nutshell, while it might seem that "the action" in Ephesus lies in the characteristics of the city that make it prominent, in fact the world-changing grace of God has been revealed in the new humanity formed in Christ. The grace of God has come to these Ephesian believers in power. The visible effect of that powerful grace is to form a radically new kind of people, the people of God in Christ.

19. *Anchor Bible Dictionary*, 2:543.

With such background in mind, we read the great benediction at the end of the first half of the book of Eph at 3:20–21 with a new understanding: "Now to him who by the power at work within us is able to accomplish abundantly far more than all we can ask or imagine, to him be glory in the church and in Christ Jesus to all generations." What is the power at work within us? It is the power of God by which these Ephesian Christians are able to demonstrate the Lordship of Christ to the world. Notice especially: "who by the power at work within us is able to accomplish far more." What is that power at work within us? It is God's grace, God's gracious activity in creating and shaping a particular kind of community.

"Wait a minute!" you might be thinking. "The word *grace* does not appear in 3:20–21. Aren't you imposing your own view on this text?" It's a fair question. "Grace" does appear in Ephesians in every chapter except chapter 5, and if you look at each of those references, most of them connect God's grace with some visible effect, with some demonstration of God's power in people's lives. The early references in chapters 1 and 2 point to God's action in the work of salvation. The "riches of his grace" brought us redemption (1:7). His grace saved us (2:5, 8). But then references to God's grace turn toward mission. God's grace commissioned Paul to share the mystery of revelation with the Gentiles (3:7–8). We find in 4:7 that "*each of us* [emphasis added] was given grace according to the measure of Christ's gift" for the sake of ministry (4:12). Our lives, individually and communally, as followers of the Lord of heaven and earth, serve to demonstrate God's redemptive purposes. Therefore, Ephesians illustrates the grace-as-power or grace-as-work (divine) that includes the well-known atonement theme, but goes beyond it to the work God does in and through believers to reach out in mission to the world.

We now turn to one more Scripture that, as I mentioned earlier, also does not use the word *grace*, but offers an important description of it.[20] It is Phil 2:12–13. First, the context: early in chapter 2 we find the

20. My understanding of this Scripture is especially beholden to John Wesley. I refer the reader to his sermon "On Working Out Our Own Salvation." It can be found in several places and formats. See http://gbgm-umc.org/umhistory/wesley/sermons/ for an online version. In print, the best source is the bicentennial edition of *The Works of John Wesley*, volume 3, 199–209. Albert C. Outler, the editor, says of the sermon, "This must be considered a landmark sermon, for it stands as the late Wesley's most complete and careful exposition of the mystery of divine-human interaction." It is through this divine-human interaction that we experience God's grace.

glorious hymn about Christ, who, though found in the form (*morphe*) of God, gave up the heavenly glory, emptied himself, and took the position of the lowest person on the socioeconomic scale—a slave. Just as Christ humbled himself, God the Father also exalted him and gave him the name above every name—"Lord." This title positions Christ above the whole cosmos—above all governments, principalities and powers. There is no place in the universe where Jesus is not Lord!

This christological hymn[21] provides the context and impetus for the exhortation that we are to have the mind of Christ (2:5). At the end of the section, in 2:12–13, we read: "Therefore, my beloved, just as you have always obeyed me, not only in my presence, but much more now in my absence,[22] *work out your* own salvation with fear and trembling; for it is God who is *at work in you, enabling you* both to will and to work for his good pleasure" (emphasis added).

We have in this injunction a critical (and challenging) linkage between our working and God's working. To stay clear of the common works-righteousness difficulty, let me quickly state that Paul is most definitely not calling for something like works righteousness. He is not telling those Philippians that they must work to earn their salvation. No, clearly Christ has already done that work, which we note from the previous verses. We might paraphrase "work out your own salvation," then, with something like, "engage actively in the salvation life until you finish (or accomplish) your work." The Greek term for "work out"—*katergazesthai*—suggests a task completed.[23] It is very close to the idea of "finish the race." As William Barclay puts it, Paul is challenging the Philippians: "Don't stop halfway; go on until the work of salvation is fully wrought out in you."[24]

21. I just lapsed into academic-speak, which may be unfamiliar to some folks. Christological refers to the doctrine of Christ. It's the standard theological term to refer to all the thinking of the church related to Christ's person and work. The idea that Phil 2:6–11 is a hymn comes from the work of biblical scholars who have recognized the rhythm and other technical characteristics of poetry, thus suggesting that maybe these verses give us a hint at an early hymn that followers of Jesus sang in worship.

22. According to Bible scholars, Paul languishes in prison while he writes this letter, hence his absence from them. But Paul has also invested deeply in this fledgling congregation and loves them dearly. Scholars also point out that the language Paul uses is filled with deep affection.

23. If Paul could have known Larry the Cable Guy, he might have been tempted to say, "Git 'er done!" which, strangely, might be a fairly good translation of *katergazesthai*, minus the slang.

24. Barclay, *Letters to the Philippians, Colossians, and Thessalonians*, 41.

We must admit, in today's climate, "work out your own salvation" probably does not make the list of favorite Bible verses to quote. No, I hear much more often another Philippians verse (4:13), "I can do all things through Christ who strengthens me," used, we must admit, to curb anxiety about some stress a person feels. Yet, here we find God's Word: "Get to work!"

If Paul had left us right there, we could understandably feel the heavy weight of obligation, but he did not. He clarifies "work out your own salvation" with, "for God is at work in you." The preposition *for* provides the logical connection between our working and God working, and puts God's work logically prior to ours. We work *because* God is already working in us. Our activity—our work—is fueled by God's action in us (God provides the ability). Our working out our own salvation makes visible (in a limited, human way, to be sure) God's goodness, holiness, grace, and mercy.

Two related verses from other books come to mind to help clarify how *our* working out *our* salvation might in some way approximate making visible the very nature of God. In Eph 4:24, we read that we are to "clothe [ourselves] with the new self, created according to the likeness of God in true righteousness and holiness." The Spirit of God gives life to the Body of Christ and empowers it with gifts to make God's nature and purposes visible. Thus, in clothing ourselves with the new self, that self has about it the likeness of God. In a limited way, we thus have the privilege of demonstrating the righteousness of God. The other verse, from Col 3:10, speaks to the same principle: "And have clothed yourselves with the new self, which is being renewed in knowledge according to the image of its creator." This verse comes in the middle of encouragement to lead a certain quality of life that exemplifies the Kingdom, the new life in Christ. It is characterized by compassion, gentleness, and meekness, just to name three of the qualities mentioned there.

This idea of the new self with its implications for a certain quality of life so goes against the grain of our bumper-sticker theology—"Christians aren't perfect, just forgiven"—we can hardly bear the responsibility. In fact, we have almost turned it into a moral principle that Christians should not only dispense with worry about "perfectionism," but we should avoid it at all cost. Perfectionism, however, simply is not the issue for today. What is the issue is that Jesus' followers are supposed to look like Jesus, in our character and our actions. When Jesus tell us, "Be perfect, therefore, as your heavenly Father is perfect" (Matt 5:48), he is not laying a perfectionist load on us, but he *is* telling us that our character is to reflect God's character, concerns, and purposes. There is no lower level Christianity to which we can retreat to let us off the hook for doing what God calls us to do. Hence the crucial importance of Phil 2:12–13: we can work out our salvation, we can *accomplish* God's redemptive purposes precisely because we do not depend on any self-generated ability. On the contrary, *God is providing the ability.*

The power for Christian living—like the power that saves us from sin—is God's grace. It is the work of God in our lives to produce the fruit of Christian maturity. Growing to maturity not only fits us for heaven, it empowers us for ministry in this world. Grace therefore sanctifies us, making us holy according to God's image restored in us and in order to serve God's purposes in the world.

I hope by now you can see why I have taken such pains to set a context around common Christian sound bites about grace so that we can get to this essential principle of Christian maturity. Because God interacts with us through grace, we find in that grace the power (ability, literally in Greek, *dunamis*) to move forward toward maturity, to embody, practice, and make visible the nature and redemptive purposes of the One who is Lord. While we are responsible to live in this way, we are not left to our own native abilities. God is already at work. And because God is at work, we don't have the option of not working.

The discussion of grace in this chapter has focused on two major points. First, I have argued that the concept of grace has been unnecessarily and unhelpfully reduced to refer almost exclusively to Christ's atoning work, with occasional and somewhat vague references to grace as divine favor. This shrunken view of grace has had a negative impact on the life of the church. Secondly, beyond the grace at work in atonement and in that threshold moment of stepping into relationship with Christ, grace sanctifies the believer, making her or him increasingly like Christ in thought, word, and action. This sanctifying work necessarily includes one's discerning one's gifts for ministry and serving sacrificially in the name and power of Christ.

I have argued, therefore, that, in general, teaching on grace in today's church has been lacking in this regard, a point that raises the question of doctrine. What does doctrine do? Here we begin to encounter that mysterious interaction between the Spirit of God and the human heart. To this question we will turn in the next chapter.

5 The Overlooked Dimension
Doctrine

> Doctrine is not an affair of the tongue, but of the life; is
> not apprehended by the intellect and memory merely,
> like other branches of learning; but is received only
> when it possesses the whole soul, and finds its seat
> and habitation in the inmost recesses of the heart.[1]

DOCTRINE GONE BAD

It probably seems odd that, since I have started all previous chapters with a quote from (mostly) John Wesley, I would now use one from John Calvin. I chose it because it shows that Calvin, too, as representative of probably the dominant Protestant doctrinal tradition in North America, cared deeply about the same concern that drove Wesley's ministry. Though these well-known leaders lived at different times and in differing contexts,[2] both understood how doctrine shapes not only our theological concepts, but also the emotional tonality of our lives. These two domains—thought and emotion—become visible in our dispositions, which, remember, are the tendencies to act in certain ways under certain conditions.

---

1. Calvin, *On the Christian Life*.

2. John Calvin lived in the 1500s and operated from Geneva, Switzerland. His life overlapped with Martin Luther's, though Calvin was more than twenty years younger than Luther. John Wesley, on the other hand, lived in the 1700s in England. In one sense, Wesley was an heir to the Protestant tradition formed by the likes of Luther and Calvin.

Doctrine therefore teaches us what to *care about*. It influences us holistically, not just intellectually, which is an understanding we have almost lost, I dare say, in our day and time. For a variety of reasons, intellectual and social forces in modern culture have contributed to the unlinking of sound doctrine and the spiritual health to which Calvin's comment above refers. To be sure, you can find lots of interest in doctrinal questions and debates. Do a search for "Christian doctrine" on the Internet, for instance, and see how many hits you get. There are plenty, which suggests a strong interest in doctrine, but for what purpose?

Among other things, doctrine is commonly understood to accomplish two important purposes. First, it teaches us *what to think* about God and the beliefs that identify us as participants in the Christian faith. Teaching us what to think puts us in proper relation to truth and, by extension, to God. This point implies that what we think about God and the Christian faith matters. You cannot believe "just any" doctrine and stand either in right relationship to truth, to God, or to other Christians. In the New Testament books called the Pastoral Letters (1, 2 Timothy and Titus), we find a number of injunctions to preach and follow sound doctrine so as to keep the faith and to avoid being led away by false teaching, which would have seriously deleterious effects on one's relation to God.

Doctrine also helps identify the particular *group to which we belong* within the Christian faith. For example, if you scan the web pages of Christian organizations, you will often find a "What We Believe" or "Our Beliefs" page, on which you find a summary of that organization's doctrinal guidelines. Doing so, one gets the sense that these groups are saying, "We hold these distinctive beliefs and practices. They are important. It's how we 'do' the faith." This function of doctrine is narrower than the former one, but widely recognized nonetheless.

In both cases, however, we see that doctrine primarily serves the purpose of establishing boundaries, either conceptual ones for truth bearing and coherence or to identify one's relationship to a particular group. If one agrees with the group's prescribed doctrines, one is properly "in." Establishing identity is a legitimate concern, if for no other reason than the practical one of helping people know what they need to believe in order to be recognized as a member. Any organization (religious or not) needs a stated purpose that names its mission and core values, its doctrines, so that people can know what kind of group they're joining.

Some groups seem to use doctrinal agreement primarily as a control measure to keep their membership regulated, even, in some sense, "pure." I appreciate the motive, but find the control measures not very effective. This practice reduces doctrine to a matter of mere intellectual agreement by which group leaders judge people's suitability for membership. It mixes the legitimate need for identity and group integrity with doctrine in such a way that only the ideas as ideas seem to matter, not how those ideas are embodied in actual life. Doctrine becomes a shibboleth in these situations. This is a most unfruitful trade-off. In our day, doctrine too often has been reduced to (as the Calvin quote says) "intellect and memory," and misses that formative power of doctrine that "possesses the whole soul." In fact, the doctrine that we truly believe—that we take to heart—does have a formative impact far beyond recognition.

Unfortunately, much controversy overshadows good and useful ideas about doctrine. Understandably, but regrettably, we Christians tend to reflect the tensions found in American political and popular culture and we often employ various parts of Christian doctrine to uphold some particular cause. Labels are always problematic, but especially in American politics, we see ones like "conservative" and "progressive." When used in relation to Christian participation in politics, people identifying themselves via such labels often bring doctrinal beliefs into the judgments about the merits of a given political position. They thereby (unwittingly) put Christian doctrine in a secondary position to their political ends. Although I believe people in such circles act this way with utmost sincerity, they do damage to Christian doctrine.[3]

The counterbalance to an over-controlling "doctrinal correctness" is to denigrate doctrine or, worse, to hide doctrines behind vague references to other values. You have possibly heard the slogan, "Doctrine divides. Love unites." At first glance, this suspicion toward doctrine appears to have Scripture on its side. You may remember the criticism the Resurrected Lord levels against the church in Ephesus: "I know your works, your toil and your patient endurance. I know that you cannot

---

3. For a perceptive analysis of this problem, see Hunter, *To Change the World*, especially pps. 101–66. Hunter describes three groups of Christians: "conservatives," "progressives," and "neo-Anabaptists," all in relation to their engagement with the political process in the United States. Although I am less confident in what he says about neo-Anabaptists, I think his description of conservatives and progressives is tellingly on the mark.

tolerate evildoers; you have tested those who claim to be apostles but are not, and have found them to be false. I also know that you are enduring patiently and are bearing up for the sake of my name, and that you have not grown weary. But I have this against you, that you have abandoned the love you had at first" (Rev 2:2–4). These verses are commonly taken to refer to a church that is doctrinally vigilant but cold and loveless. Remember another aphorism often aimed at loveless doctrinal correctness: "People don't care how much you know until they know how much you care."

I appreciate the motive not to use doctrine as either a whip to secure agreement or a bar to block entrance. If we draw boundaries too narrowly, we unnecessarily and tragically carve up the Body of Christ. But "doctrine divides, love unites"—a statement usually offered without qualification— actually makes a claim that can be tested. Does doctrine always divide? Of course not. Because doctrine helps identify shared values, it is as likely to unite as it is to divide.

A third (and very popular) way to handle doctrine is to reduce it to "practical principles." In this case people might even avoid using the word *doctrine* because it is so commonly taken to refer only to abstract, academic (therefore irrelevant to real life) ideas. Americans are very pragmatic. We gravitate toward "what works." People who think they don't like doctrine often do like practical, real-world principles that they can employ in daily living. Here we find a rather dismissive attitude toward "theology" or, at least, a willingness to hurry through the seemingly academic abstractions that provide the necessary framework so that we can get to "the good stuff" of real-life practicalities. "The doctrine of the Trinity? Oh, yeah, we all agree with that. Now, tell me how I can pray more effectively or get out of debt or be a good parent."

Once again we find ourselves facing a "such a time as this" moment. From practically every research source you can name—anyone asking Americans about their religious beliefs or, more distantly, knowledge about religious beliefs—we find that American Christians are pitifully ignorant. We mix karma and reincarnation with Christian teachings about resurrection, blending ideas that don't blend. So here is a supreme irony: in our rush for finding "what works," it turns out that almost nothing works to help us grow to maturity, because we have lost track of this goal altogether. We do not know how to identify the goal, which is, in large part, the problem of lack of doctrinal awareness. Far too many

Christians seem to be on a quest for the good spiritual life without any useful means to gauge whether or not they are actually making progress in that desired direction.[4]

DOCTRINE AND ITS SOMETIMES CONFUSING SYNONYMS

Given the context described above, it is no wonder that people suffer confusion about the nature, purpose, and function of Christian doctrine. Often, when people get mired in debates about doctrine, other words surface, usually with negative tones, as in bumper-sticker statements like, "My karma ran over my dogma." Terms like "dogma," "creed," and "theology" surface in comments from often frustrated Christians about current conditions in the church. How is doctrine—especially as I use it in this chapter—related to but distinct from these terms? Let me clarify them and then we'll be ready to delve specifically into the heart-shaping force of doctrine.

"Dogma" comes directly from the Greek language and, in Christian scholarship, it generally refers to the standard, authoritative beliefs that identify and guide a group. In our day, few people use "dogma" because of heavily negative connotations. They would probably talk about "our beliefs" or "our doctrines," perhaps even "core values," but, when talking about what distinguishes them from other groups, they probably should use "dogma" more than they do. Usually within a group, dogma is settled, not up for discussion. If you were to look at a Greek lexicon, you would see that the word *doctrine* appears as a synonym, but other terms there, like "ordinance" and "decree," help us see the relatively fixed nature of dogma. It serves to provide the conceptual boundaries of the faith. An example of Christian dogma is the Trinity. Christians claim that God is, by nature, Trinity: Father, Son, and Holy Spirit.[5] If you're going to believe what (the vast majority of) Christians believe, your belief system will include some notion of God as Trinity.

---

4. One example of the dearth of doctrinal awareness coming to light recently is that evangelical Christians are almost as likely as non-evangelical Christians to believe that there are more ways to salvation than through Jesus alone.

5. Our earlier discussion about Jesus' death on the cross connects deeply to the doctrine of the Trinity, perhaps the most complex and challenging aspect of Christian teaching, but also the most fundamental.

"Dogma" raises the specter of dogmatism. A dogmatic person comes across as rigid, unbending, unwilling to consider other people's ideas, closed-minded. Of course, people can be narrow, closed-minded, "dogmatic," but that problem has more to do with people's attempt to exercise control than it does the actual content of religious beliefs. If, for example, I refuse to explore a theological idea with you because "my mind is made up," the problem lies not so much in the particular doctrinal conviction I hold, but rather in my attempt to maintain some sort of control by not discussing it with you. Dogmatism reveals a psychological attitude more than it does the actual content of ideas.[6]

Neither is Christian dogma arbitrary, something people "just made up," another charge critics often level at this term.[7] Dogmas didn't just drop into the church's thinking from nowhere. They have come through a process of sifting, challenge, and acceptance over time. Again, belief in God as Trinity is a good example. You don't find the word *Trinity* in the New Testament, but you start to see the concept there (check 2 Cor 13:13, for example). And, to anticipate a later point about creeds, the dogma of the Trinity came to be summarized in two of the church's most well-known creeds, the Apostles' and the Nicene, even though neither creed uses the word *Trinity*.[8] We regard the Trinity as essential to our understanding of God's nature, but it took awhile for the Church to get to this point, and it came not without controversy.[9]

Dogmas are, therefore, general and basic beliefs that have gone through a process of forming and testing, eventually being determined by church leaders as universally true and authoritative for faithful Christian

6. Admittedly, there are ways that dogma can promote dogmatism. A dogmatic claim may call for one to avoid having contact with a certain kind of person. But generally, with regard to the doctrines, we focus on the ideas and related practices that help people live as faithful Christians rather than on dogmatic boundaries.

7. This allegation provides the main thesis for all the Dan Brown novels turned into films like *The DaVinci Code*. Politically powerful leaders in the church's early centuries established "orthodox" doctrine by sheer force and engaged in cover-ups that marginalized the Gnostics and hid the truth. I am surprised at how many intelligent people take this superficially plausible but easily refutable claim as utter truth.

8. Tertullian, one of the early third-century church fathers, used the Latin *trinitas* along with *personae* (persons) and *substantia* (substance) in order to capture the essence of the Three-in-One God's nature.

9. At various times during church history, people have risen to question the doctrine: Arius in the fourth century (which helped bring about the Nicene Creed), Socinus in the sixteenth century and, today, if you see a Unitarian Church, these folks deny the Trinity.

belief and practice. For the same reasons, dogma has been organized into a coherent system of authoritative statements, which we now take as starting points for understanding our faith.[10]

"Creed" is another term that people sometimes don't like because of its guilt-by-association connection with formalism and slavish adherence to tradition. The same prejudice that makes people not like "dogma" drives a similar antipathy to this term. If one wants to be "spiritual" without being "religious," then a "creed" seems unnecessarily limiting, even oppressive. Those of us with a pietistic frame of mind criticize the formalism of reciting creeds without engaging the heart.

Today, with significant confusion surrounding what "being a Christian" actually means, creeds serve an especially important and timely function. A creed summarizes the faith in a helpful way and, like dogma, helps people grasp the basic beliefs of the group to which they belong. The word *creed* comes from the Latin *credo* (I believe). Saying a creed means that one affirms that not only does one agree with the basic beliefs of the Christian faith, but one also commits oneself to live according to these beliefs. A creed therefore is a summary statement of the authoritative beliefs that Christians hold, beliefs that bind us together and guide the way we live. The Apostles' Creed is probably the best-known example. Christians across a wide spectrum of denominations and communities say the creed. This agreement helps identify the Body of Christ, even if we disagree on other matters.

"Theology" is yet another term in our list of often-misunderstood words. How does it differ from "doctrine"? At its base, "theology" means "reasoning" or "thinking" about God (literally, from the Greek, *theology* is a combination of the words *God* and *word*). In one sense, then, "theology" covers broad territory. If you ever think about your relationship with God or the nature and work of God, you're doing theology.

---

10. Describing the human, historical process by which dogmas came into existence raises questions about divine revelation and inspiration. How, if at all, was God involved in the formation of these beliefs? To delve very far into these questions goes beyond our aim here, but let me say that making reference to the human and historical part of this process in no way weakens the sense about God's guidance and oversight of the formation of dogma. In fact, one of the amazing characteristics about Christian theology is that it proclaims a God who works within actual history. Thus, I want to acknowledge the divine side even though we won't explore it here. This point will take on more relevance and importance later in the chapter. With this qualification, let's move on to the other "problem" words associated with "doctrine."

One example I often use to illustrate how we all do theology involves intercessory prayer. If you're standing at the bedside of a friend in the hospital and you pray for that friend, what do you say in your prayer? You might ask God to heal the friend, or to be with the friend, to guide doctors' and nurses' hands in attending to your friend. Notice what the prayer assumes. If you ask God to heal, then you evidently believe that God has both the ability and the will to heal. Whether God does so through normal medical or supernatural means, you still have a set of theological assumptions active in your prayer. In praying, you've "done theology." You're probably not concentrating on the nature and purposes of God when you pray, but you have a set of theological convictions at work, nonetheless.

If this is the case, then why do so many people preface a remark with, "Well, I'm not a theologian, but . . ."? Why does the word *theology* have so much baggage? In part it has to do with the technical jargon associated with the guild of professional or academic theologians. Almost all of this language remains completely obscure to normal Christians.[11] The reason why such language comes into play is completely understandable, once you think about it. Academics are experts in their fields of study. They know better than the average Christian the complexities of the questions that theological statements answer. Paradoxically and perhaps ironically, this highly technical language develops for the purpose of precision and clarity—people who have studied in great detail and realize the complexities of theological topics seek just the right word or phrase to capture what they are trying to describe. Academics love "nuance."

One unhappy result is that "theology" has been taken away from the people of God and is now too much the reserved domain of professionals in the academy. The experts focus on analyzing claims and arguments for the purpose of establishing validity and coherence. This work is sometimes called second-order theology, because it deals more (somewhat ironically) with methodological and technical concerns than with God per se. The nature of this work is exploratory and self-critical. But it is highly technical and only people schooled in the academic discipline can participate fully in the debates.

The theology that everyday believers practice in prayer and worship and Bible study, on the other hand, is often called first-order theology,

11. Actually, any field has a lingo. I am almost completely lost when my "techie" computer-savvy friends start discussing some latest technological tidbit.

because it deals more directly with the practical interactions between Christians and God. When in the act of praying or worshipping, for example, we do not normally interrupt these activities to analyze our beliefs. We simply pray and worship. We are "believing in action," putting our convictions about God's nature and purposes to work in daily life. We are therefore engaging in theological work. We are doing theology. It is every bit as much doing theology as the academic theologian does.[12] I hope that any reader who struggles with the idea that she or he is a theologian will begin to accept the call of every follower of Jesus to engage deeply in sustained theological reflection.

Thinking this way about theology, we can see that when we engage in intercessory prayer or virtually any other Christian practice, we are actually putting doctrine to work. We are practicing what we actually believe. We have certain beliefs about God's nature that call for certain attitudes and actions. And, at this point, we can see that I should not overstate the distinctions that I have been making between "dogma," "creed," "theology" and "doctrine."

Nonetheless, because I think far too many Christians do not understand what "doctrine" means, nor its critical relevance for vital Christian faith, I reserve a certain domain for the term, which I will shortly examine. Here we anticipate what is coming. Doctrine has to do with the nature and purposes of God and the way we Christians embody and realize those purposes in everyday life. In fact, theology is a matter of the heart.

The terms I have defined above have important uses in the church's life. "Dogma" sets boundaries and helps identify the followers of a religion. "Creed" summarizes what a wide number of those believers actually believe and seek to live. "Theology" does the work of testing and revising. Still, these important functions do not adequately cover our particular concern with doctrine. If we lump doctrine in with these other terms, we do our faith a disservice.

THE HEART-SHAPING IMPACT OF DOCTRINE

The term "doctrine," like "creed," comes from the Latin, *doctrina*, which means "teaching" or "instruction." In Latin, a teacher is a *doctor*, and you can see this word's connection to doctrine. At its basis, then, doctrine

---

12. When the academic theologian prays and worships, she or he is on the same plane as the normal, everyday believer, only with a bigger vocabulary.

is simply instruction for Christian living. Sound (true, life-giving) doctrine maintains and nourishes the deep connection between God's nature and purposes and the way we conduct our lives. It does so by engaging the whole person—thoughts, desires, dispositions, and actions. In other words, doctrine properly understood engages the heart.

This view stands in sharp contrast to the conventional ones I described at the beginning of this chapter. It is time to close the gap between ideas—to which we may give rational agreement, but which do not affect the way we live—and the dispositions to act which ultimately show the true character of our discipleship. The ideas that actually drive our behavior are, in fact, the doctrines we actually believe. Not only do we believe them intellectually, but, in some ways, we also "feel" them. We start making problems for ourselves when we disengage doctrine from life, and when we do, we should fully expect our Lord to say, "This people honors me with their lips, but their hearts are far from me."

Doctrine therefore has a way of shining the light on our true and deepest desires, which, in turn, become visible in our goals and behaviors. It reminds me of Jesus' teaching about treasures, that where our treasures lie, there we will find our hearts. For this reason, I find Henry Knight's twofold definition (which he borrows from John Wesley, who borrows it from another source) particularly illuminating. He refers to doctrine as "descriptive accounts of *the nature of God and of the Christian life*"[13] (emphasis added).

I like this definition for two main reasons. First, in using the word *descriptive*, it does not overstate the role of doctrine. Knight could have used "normative" rather than "descriptive," but, in doing so, he would have moved the term closer to what we typically mean when we use the word *dogma*. "Descriptive" permits, it seems to me, a wider range of legitimate options that recognizes the possibility of error and allows for correction. With regard to the aim of spiritual maturity, for example, Protestant Christians from the Wesleyan-Arminian and Reformed-Calvinist traditions disagree on how far the vision for sanctification can be applied this side of heaven and glorification for a believer. Thinking of doctrine as descriptive rather than normative allows for conversation, cooperation, and mutual growth across groups who might otherwise feel constrained to protect dogmatic boundaries.

13. Knight, *Presence of God in the Christian Life*, 163.

Second, this definition of doctrine holds together theology and life, thus countering the tendency to pull these domains apart. Doctrine seeks to describe the nature and purposes of God, our fundamental reference point. Here we see the overlap between the terms "theology" and "doctrine." To think doctrinally, we must think theologically. But we must not let the work remain here, for it necessarily leads to the second part—the Christian life, the way we actually live. Doctrine describes how followers of Jesus engage in the life of discipleship.

To aim at the fullness of Christian maturity, therefore, one must engage in doctrinal work that integrates ideas and practice. We cannot simply jump from one to the other, however. To do so would be to lapse back into that two-step process I criticized back in chapter 2, which assumes that if one understands the concept one can then practice it. If doctrine sheds light on desires and dispositions to act, which I believe it does, then we need to attend to the very mental ground that we too often overlook. This step takes us into the hard work of gaining awareness about the emotional tonality of doctrine, in order to move forward into the actual practice of doctrinal truth.

I admit that I am pressing an idea here that may seem strange or even confused. I am arguing that thoughts and feelings *always* interact at some level and that, for the sake of growing to maturity, we should pay attention to this dynamic interaction much more than we do. In the most cerebral of thoughts, we are feeling something, even if unaware of our emotions at that moment. From the Bible's perspective on the heart, this is how human nature works.

My claim here thus requires that we think again about thinking. What exactly are we doing when we are thinking? The information processing metaphor that stems from the ubiquitous presence of computer technology has done much to hide the fact that when we think, we are doing more than merely cognitively processing ideas. Even though, when thinking occupies our consciousness (when we are thinking "about" something) we are often not aware of our emotions, those emotions still contribute to thinking in a practical way.

In the paragraphs to follow, we will move step by step through a series of examples to illustrate this crucial point about the inherent connection between thoughts, emotions, and dispositions to act. In due time, we will aim specifically at how these mental experiences connect to Christian doctrine. One word of caution: It is easy, on hearing the word *emotion,* mentally to jump immediately to some obvious feeling-laden situation, like the angry gesture of a motorist cut off in traffic or the tearful embraces of long-separated friends. Such moments clearly have strong emotional tones and we recognize them as such. The work we will do below is not so obvious, but nonetheless real and important. As I have done elsewhere, I will often use the term "emotionally tonal" or "emotional tonality" to refer to this more subtle presence of emotion mixed with cognition.

To practice recognizing emotional tonality, consider, for example, a word like "confident." You have studied hard, paid attention in class, and prepared diligently for the examination tomorrow. You feel confident that you will score well. Now, what goes into this feeling of confidence? In part, it has to do with the consequence of good, diligent, preparation. Likewise, one may feel confident because one has had previous positive experience with taking examinations in this class. Confidence thus has a cognitive component: "I have studied hard. I know the material. I am ready." Confidence anticipates a positive outcome. But along with the logic of these thoughts goes an emotionally tonal response. Being confident feels good.

Now let's look at emotional tonality in relation to real-life experiences. Let's say that you have double-booked your appointment schedule and you now have two very important, but conflicting, items on your calendar. The people you need to meet are exceedingly busy and protective of their time. It took a lot of work and time on your part to get these appointments. Having to reschedule with either one, on first glance, looks devastatingly counterproductive to your goals for the appointments in the first place. You obviously cannot be at both places at the same time and you also don't want to miss either one or offend the people you've scheduled to meet. In other words, you have a real dilemma on your hands and the stakes are high.

Imagine yourself in this situation. What mental experiences come to mind? While you're thinking, "How am I going to solve this problem?" you also probably feel something like a little bit of panic. You might have to fight the temptation to answer, "I can't!" This "not solvable" feeling probably lies just below the level of consciousness, because you are focused on the external situation (the schedule conflict) and not your own mental processes, but it is present and powerful nonetheless. But you don't succumb to the temptation to give up because you know you must find a solution. The appointments are too important and the stakes too high not to figure it out. So, you start to rifle through the options: whom to call, what to say, what alternatives to suggest, how you'll apologize, and so on.

Then comes the breakthrough moment when it appears that you hit upon a solution. You mentally work through it, checking and refining until you become confident (notice the word) it really does solve the problem. You make the necessary calls and the matter is settled. The burden has lifted and you breathe a sigh of relief.

Notice the emotional tonality of this experience. It has taken me three paragraphs to describe what usually happens in a few blinks of the eye. You could have this experience sitting in a busy coffee shop and, though you are, in a sense, suffering, no one around you knows what is going on in your mind. But for you this experience has been like a storm of thoughts and feelings. You had to concentrate on the salient points of the situation, which made you momentarily unaware of feelings, until, perhaps, at the end of it, when you could then relax and think about what just happened.

Notice, furthermore, that your thoughts and emotions "matched," so to speak. When you first discover the schedule conflict, you quickly realize (cognitively) that you have made a grave mistake. Immediately connected to the idea "mistake," you "feel" another idea, perhaps captured by the word *alarm* because the problem represents danger to your goals. That emotionally tonal thought comes, in a sense logically, as an inference from the first idea, "I have made a mistake." Probably by this time, the flood of feelings has hit: fear, frustration, anger, self-reproach, or a number of other possible emotions. But notice, too, these feelings involve thoughts and thoughts, and feelings seem to mirror each other.

I stated in chapter 2 on the heart, that feelings are "about" something and this situation of the schedule conflict illustrates the directionality of our emotions.[14] The feelings relate to an actual situation external to your subjective consciousness. It represents a real problem that demands solution. Failure to solve it means failure to realize an important goal. So, in a way, the feelings you have in association with the problem "make sense." The emotions contribute, furthermore, to solving the problem.

---

14. Sometimes emotions are probably not cognitive in the way I describe them here. We can also have feelings that seemingly come from nowhere and are connected to nothing. I am dealing here with what Paul Griffiths refers to as the "higher cognitive emotions." See Griffiths, *What Emotions Really Are*, 100–36.

They block out extraneous thoughts about irrelevant matters and help you concentrate on the problem at hand. They bring to the forefront of your mind the salient features of the situation that demand your attention. In these ways the emotions contribute to your thinking and help you resolve the dilemma.

In using this little story of the schedule conflict, I have left one significant factor unstated and, as yet, unexamined. I have not yet shown how thoughts and feelings relate to one's disposition, and disposition is very important for my argument in this chapter as it relates to the impact of doctrine on spiritual maturity. One's disposition—as the tendency to act in certain ways under certain conditions—also manifests emotional tonality. A number of factors, including doctrinal ideas, relationships and situational experiences shape one's disposition over time.

When we start exploring our dispositions, we can see how doctrine thus contributes both to thinking and feeling. Over time we develop tendencies to think, feel, and act in certain ways. (To the degree that doctrine faithfully reflects the nature and purposes of God, we believe that the Spirit of God uses it to shape our hearts—thoughts, feelings, and dispositions—in a God-ward direction.) Doctrine helps us engage and put into practice not only what we think but also what we *care about*. In other words, at least on the matters that concern us in this book, we *feel* what we think about, but not necessarily in ways that we immediately recognize.

Let's go back to the same scenario, then, and show how disposition can dramatically affect the outcome. The person in the situation as I sketched it managed to find a workable solution, but, in real life, it does not always turn out that way. What if the person had previously experienced a run of difficult cicumstances? Perhaps he is living through one of those seasons when every decision has led to failed plans and frustration of goals. Let's say that the two critical appointments are actually job interviews and the subject of our little story has tried and failed repeatedly to find a job. If this situation has lasted long enough, the anxiety this person feels might well up so high that, rather than working to find a solution, he might actually be frozen into inactivity. He might decide to skip either appointment. Concluding that "things always work out this way for me," he might give up in despair.

This new wrinkle in the story illustrates how both thoughts and emotions influence our dispositions. Remember that disposition refers to the characteristic tendency to act in certain ways under certain conditions. It depends on a person's viewpoint or interpretation of the salient features of a situation—those one finds the most important. In other words, our understanding of the details of the situation plays an important role. But understanding does not operate alone. The emotional pressure of the situation impinges upon the understanding and calls for some kind of action. *How we respond* relates integrally to how thoughts and feelings have been shaped over time by the myriad forces and pressures—intellectual and otherwise—that go into training our tendencies to act, for good or ill.

More or less everything I have described in the double-booking dilemma above applies to spiritual growth. Imagine your hunger for intimate relationship with God. (I trust this hunger is not too hard to imagine.) On its face, it has no apparent connection to doctrine, as we typically understand that term. That is to say, if you feel hunger to know God, you probably do not immediately think, "I need to study theology."[15] No, to satisfy the hunger, you likely would search for a resource on some spiritual practice, like prayer, which has evident connections to the hunger you feel. So, you find a book on prayer and you begin to anticipate the benefit you expect to get from reading it. That sense of anticipation is a form of hope. Notice therefore the emotional tonality of your attitude as you begin to read. In the process of reading, this book serves as one means by which you engage a matter that you *care about*. Cognitively, you can identify and explain how and why the topic is significant, but you also feel the pull of a desired outcome.

As you read, you hit upon a comment that evokes one of those "Aha!" moments. You have the feeling of discovery, of clarification, of deepened understanding. Normally, in such a moment we do not first pay attention to emotions because the content of the insightful idea holds our attention. Given the cognitive work you are doing, it may seem like nothing more than your intellect, your understanding, doing the work. Emotions are active, nonetheless. The new insight might feel exhilarating, liberating, exciting, comforting or challenging, but since you're concentrating on other things you probably do not notice the emotional tonality of the thoughts.

Once you start to notice the link between thoughts, emotions, and action, you can see the pervasive nature of this integrated experience, even where you would not expect to find it. Consider, for example, the

---

15. Generically, "theology" refers to the study of or teaching about God.

discipline of philosophy, which, by any measure, appears to be the most cerebral of activities, therefore the least amenable to emotions. Alvin Plantinga, one of this generation's most eminent philosophers, has written extensively in the philosophy of religion, particularly in relation to the rationality of faith.[16] The following quote, which comes from his book *Warranted Christian Belief*, describes the *intellectual experience* of one who exhibits faith, but notice as well the emotional tonality of the description: "The person with faith . . . not only believes the central claims of the Christian faith; she also (paradigmatically) finds the whole scheme of salvation enormously attractive, delightful, moving, a source of amazed wonderment."[17] *Attractive. Delightful. Moving.* Remember, Professor Plantinga is describing the response of faith to claims that one comes to believe are true, so it appears, according to the usual way of construing such situations, to be a moment of intellectual insight. And it is. But the intellect does not act alone. The terms in this description also carry significant emotional tone. We typically do not associate feelings with this complex intellectual activity, but, upon consideration, we can see them at work. Therefore, the terms in the quote also capture the emotionally tonal character of the kind of intellectual work that Christians do in expressing faith.

Sound doctrine is not (or should not be), therefore, a mere *head trip*, to use an old cliché. It is beautiful, moving, compelling, and life-giving. Doctrine properly understood captures the heart and moves the will. It is converting and transformative. It changes us, especially as we reflect on it again and again over time. In truth, this experience is (or has the possibility of being) supremely intellectual and emotionally moving, though mysterious. While a person feels that her mind has been illuminated with powerful truth, she finds it thrilling in a profound way.

Of course, not every time we encounter a doctrinal idea do we feel great swells of emotion. However, if we develop the practice of engaging doctrine prayerfully and with willing and receptive hearts, we do find that, over time, we start to feel differently. Our attitudes, our basic dispositions toward people and their situations begin to change in a Christ-ward direction. By this means, the disparate and sometimes conflicting desires

16. There is a long tradition of argument within a strand of Enlightenment-based thought that claims that religious faith is inherently irrational. Plantinga has done as much as anyone in the present day to refute this claim.

17. Plantinga, *Warranted Christian Belief*, 292.

and dreams of our lives, over time, begin to integrate into characteristics that reflect the very nature and purposes of God. From this formational process flow actions consistent with the mindset. In other words, if the doctrine with which we are interacting is sound, the actions will generally reflect biblical truth. Our lives will embody the love of God and neighbor so manifestly present in Jesus' life and teachings.

Here, admittedly, the situation becomes even more complex than my description shows. It depends on a combination of self-awareness, willingness to change, and courage to persevere. A moment of insight may develop into new behavior more reflective of Christ's nature, or it may not, depending on other conditions and forces at work. My description assumes, for example, a sufficient degree of humility, in other words, openness to change one's mind and actions. With reference to the example of reading a book to engage a hunger for intimacy with God, part of our challenge is to develop the practice of self-awareness as we read. Many Christians read regularly on topics related to Christian discipleship. Some people simply love to read and they devour whatever they can get their hands on. Sometimes we confuse *reading about* with *doing something about*. Yet reading alone (even reading much) does not automatically translate into changed behavior. As we read, are we aware of our desires and dispositions? As we read, how are we responding to ideas that provoke and challenge us? Are we open to change?[18]

This is why thinking about disposition is so important. Disposition has to do with what we *care about*, what we think about and value. Disposition takes time to develop. It must be practiced. Changes in our dispositions require attending to the full range of mental activities associated with both thought and emotion. It means that we need to practice noticing how we respond emotionally to teaching, relationships, and other experiences. This process shows the way our hearts actually work and, with practice, we can grow more effectively toward maturity.

Now let us turn to specific doctrinal concerns which have already appeared in this book and which I think lie at the heart of many of our difficulties with growth toward maturity. Using these topics, I intend to

---

18. In addition to an open, humble attitude, then, we also need loving Christian friends who see our blinds spots and thereby help us to overcome unconscious or semi-conscious resistance to change. In the community of a small group, for example, the Spirit of God uses life-giving doctrine to provoke, challenge, heal, and stimulate growth. We will address the corporate dimension of spiritual maturity in the next chapter.

develop my claim that doctrine not only helps us know what to think but also, in some sense, how to feel. It helps us know what to care about.[19]

Earlier I complained about how sound bite slogans regarding the atonement ("Jesus died for my sins") and about Christmas ("Happy Birthday, Jesus") woefully underestimate the actual work of salvation to which people who use these statements laudably intend to point. Of course, I recognize that many people who use these slogans think about much more than what is captured in them. Nonetheless, because these statements are so common and because they serve as shorthand renditions of the Christian faith, they in fact do exercise an unintended yet spiritually debilitating influence in the Christian subculture.

The summary statement, "Jesus died for my sins," relates most explicitly to that view of the atonement commonly called the penal substitutionary view. Christ takes our place on the cross and, in suffering and dying, he pays the penalty for our sin. By virtue of this great act, and on the condition of our trust in Christ, God forgives us, graciously declares us righteous in Christ and brings us into a new relationship with God. This summary emphasizes matters of profound and critical importance, yet observe how the terms refer to that which lies external to the conditions of our hearts. With so much emphasis on the atonement as dealing with our *status* before God (guilty sinners now forgiven and made redeemed saints[20]), and with very little corresponding awareness of our sin-sickened ontological *condition*, we do not sufficiently understand what Christ has actually accomplished in our salvation. The penal substitutionary view therefore tells only part of the story that we need to know for the fullness of Christian life.

Part of the reason for a shrunken understanding of the atonement relates, ironically, to the paltry celebrations of Christmas that remain so

19. As a by-product to this process, I ask readers to notice the deeply integrated, interrelated character of the historic faith's core doctrines. They stand and fall together. This characteristic illustrates the power and usefulness of creeds that summarize the church's core beliefs.

20. With regard to the word *saint*, we see a corresponding difficulty in how to understand Christian holiness. One of the arguments between Calvinist/Reformed Christians and Wesleyan-Arminian Christians revolves around the degree to which the "set-apartness" associated with holiness is positional and missional (we are holy by virtue of our relationship to Christ and our call to serve God's purposes in the world) or also ontological (we actually become holy, like Christ). The debate has hardened these positions over the years.

narrowly focused on Jesus' birth (i.e., "Happy Birthday, Jesus"). This practice elides the impact of the atonement in tragic but unrecognized ways. It likewise shapes our emotionally tonal thoughts, our dispositions. In other words, the cumulative impact of the formulaic representations of the core of the Gospel directly affects what we *care about*. In turn, this doctrinal impoverishment affects the church's ministry. It leads to a less than adequate witness in the world.

Rather than "Happy Birthday, Jesus," then, what would it do for more Christians to spend more time *thinking about* God becoming human, about the Incarnation of the Word of God? How would such reflection shape our dispositions? How would it affect what we *care about*? Pondering the Incarnation challenges us to think about the question I have asked previously, related to the atonement: *what kind of person* would do such a thing, to die for the sins of the world? Romans 5:10 reminds us, Christ died for us while we were enemies of God. Jesus' death is not a mere heroic death, therefore, like that of the soldiers in *Saving Private Ryan*. They died saving a compatriot's life for a good cause. Jesus died for his enemies in what looks like, from a strictly human viewpoint, a hopeless cause. What kind of person would do such a thing?

Only a supremely loving, merciful, all-powerful God who determines to save the world by a peculiar—to say the least—display of power. Jesus as God Incarnate reveals God's power by dying and rising from the dead. The kind of person who would do such a thing says something not only about God, but also about humans and the human predicament. As Phil 2 tells us, the One who shares God's nature and glory emptied himself of that glory and took our human nature, receiving the effects of our sin-sickness in order to heal us and to conquer sin. In addition to paying the penalty for sin, therefore, Jesus addresses the ontological problem of sin. God does something *for us* by forgiving and restoring relationship. God does something in us by healing and liberating us from the power of sin.

Pondering the Incarnation thus enriches our understanding of the nature and impact of the Atonement. Together they teach us about God's intention for human existence in a way that common simplifications about either Jesus' death or his birth do not. They thus point us toward the doctrine of *sanctification*, toward examining the envisioned and expected characteristics of life in Christ. If we do not also recognize what God has done and is doing—via the Spirit's activity—*in us*, we do not yet realize the full extent of salvation. And here we have the old problem—to use language of an earlier generation—of Jesus as Savior, but not yet Lord.[21]

Which leads us to thinking about the role of the Holy Spirit in the Christian life. Although the Pentecostal and Charismatic movements in our day have certainly raised awareness of the Person and Work of the Holy Spirit, still, for most Christians, the Third Person of the Trinity has received surprisingly insufficient attention. I can only speak illustratively here, referring to broad outlines, yet, in so doing, we get at least a glimpse of God's expectation for us. A brief survey of the New Testament[22] shows, first, the relationship of Jesus to the Spirit, which is a pattern for our relationship to the Spirit as well. Second, it reveals how followers of Jesus individually and collectively exhibit the character of Christ.

Consider the following snapshots of the Spirit's work. First, we see the Spirit coming upon Mary as the originating source of Jesus' birth (Luke 1:35; Matt 1:20). The Spirit settles on Jesus in his baptism (Mark 1:10; Matt 3:16; Luke 3:22).[23] Then we find the Spirit driving Jesus into the wilderness to face his temptation (Mark 1:12; Matt 4:1; Luke 4:1). Although Mark does not expand on what happened there, the Matthean and Lukan accounts show Jesus grappling with the nature of his relationship to God and of his mission.[24] In the synagogue in Nazareth, Jesus chooses the passage from Isaiah 61 which proclaims, "The Spirit of the Lord is upon me" and summarizes his mission. Jesus then announces, "Today, this Scripture has been fulfilled in your hearing," (Luke 4:21). We

---

21. I remember as a college student in the 1970s hearing this description often. Campus Crusade for Christ, for example, in those days used two distinct tracts: the Four Spiritual Laws for leading people to faith in Christ, then another tract that introduced people to the work of the Holy Spirit. This practice coincided with the distinction often made in those days between *Spirit-filled* Christians and *carnal* Christians. Many forces then at work impinged upon this construction, which I cannot name here, but it represents a particular view of the Holy Spirit in the Christian life popularized at that time.

22. The presence and work of the Spirit in the Old Testament obviously provides essential and important material as well.

23. Some readers may know of the adoptionist Christology that suggests that Jesus "became" the Son of God by virtue of God's declaration at Jesus' baptism. I reject that notion.

24. When the Devil says, "If you are the Son of God, command these stones to become loaves of bread," we should picture Jesus struggling with the implications of being God's Son. If we believe, according to Heb 4:15, that Jesus was tempted (or tested) as we are, then this temptation for Jesus was real. He *felt* it and struggled with accepting his mission to die. I realize the questions this view raises.

can read Jesus' entire ministry, therefore, through this lens of the Spirit's activity, even without constant reference to the Spirit.

Regarding the Spirit's work in the lives of Jesus' disciples, our second point, we do well to consider Jesus' teaching about the Holy Spirit in the Gospel of John during the Last Supper scene. The numerous references by Jesus to the Spirit show that the Spirit guides and teaches believers in truth and that, in so doing, the Spirit abides in the believers (John 14:17, 25; 16:13). The Spirit bears witness to the significance of Jesus' life and ministry, both to Jesus' followers and to the world (John 15:26; 16:7–15). Likewise, it is John's Gospel that shows the Risen Christ breathing upon the disciples and commanding them to receive the Holy Spirit for the purpose of carrying on Jesus' ministry (John 20:22).

From there we can turn to the abundance of teachings about the work of the Spirit in believers individually and in the Church. In Acts 1:8 we see that Jesus links the presence of the Holy Spirit in believers with the power to be effective witnesses. The work of the Spirit in the apostolic communities is a key theme in the book of Acts. In Romans, the Spirit witnesses with our Spirits that we are children of God and joint heirs with Jesus, in contrast to the spirit of bondage found in the world (8:15–16). This witness of the Spirit gives us confidence of our standing and condition with God, and it prepares us to suffer for Christ's sake (8:17). Furthermore, in Rom 12, 1 Cor 12, Eph 4, and 1 Pet 4, we find varying lists of gifts given by the Holy Spirit to the Church so that the Church can embody the Gospel, witness effectively to Christ as Lord, and engage in his mission in the world.

Backing up from the references showing the Spirit's work in the Church's ministry, we also see substantial teachings on the Spirit's work in individual believers to make us holy, that is, to give evidence of the character of Christ in us. Several such references fall side by side, as it were, with exhortations about ministry and intertwine with them. Thus, in Rom 12 we see injunctions to love our brothers and sisters without hypocrisy, to display mutual affection, to exercise patience in suffering, to bless those who persecute us, to live in harmony with all people so far as we are able, not to be too wise in our own eyes, but to regard others as more important than ourselves. In Rom 14 we read about how more mature believers are to relate to brothers and sisters weak in the faith. In fact, from Rom 12 to the end of the book, we find extensive teachings on how Christians are to live in the present age. All of these attitudes and behaviors flow from the Spirit's work in order to accomplish God's intentions in and through us.

Likewise in 1 Cor 12 and following: since the Spirit has formed us into the one Body of Christ, we exercise certain dispositions that reflect Christ's nature. We regard each other's gifts as crucial to the health of the whole Body (12–26). In Eph 4:22ff. we see that one of the main results of the gifts of the Spirit involves exchanging the old life for the new: "You were taught to put away your former way of life, your old self, corrupt and deluded by its lusts, and to be renewed in the spirit of your minds, and to clothe yourselves with the new self, created according to the likeness of God in true righteousness and holiness." Finally, as we noted in the chapter on grace, Phil 2:12–13 teaches that God works in us (the Spirit's work) such that, by God's grace, we both desire and are enabled to work for God's good pleasure.

We could continue the search for references of the Spirit's work and find many, many more in the Scriptures. Hopefully, I have offered enough here to demonstrate the critical importance of the Spirit's role in sanctification. Once again we confront the formative power of doctrine. Doctrine teaches us not only *what to think*, but also what to *care about*. Under the Spirit's hand, doctrine shapes our dispositions and prompts actions that reflect the heart of Christ. As we grow to maturity, the goal of that growth is to produce Christ-like character in every believer, so that the Church can fruitfully undertake its mission.

We can likewise see, perhaps now more clearly, the unhappy consequences of the way doctrine is handled in popular American Christianity. We unnecessarily and very unhelpfully individualize the Gospel—"Jesus died for my sins." We focus the glory of Jesus' atoning work too narrowly on questions of guilt and punishment, coupled with concerns about status with God and future destiny. What does this teaching guide us to care about? Ourselves, getting ourselves "right with God" and, for some people who care about evangelism, doing what we can to get others right with God.

Again we turn to how doctrine teaches people what to care about. I contend that to hear repeatedly and consistently over time this small slice of teaching on the atonement, people learn to think about atonement through these terms. Our language is not emotionally neutral on this matter. If people think that this common teaching about the meaning of Jesus' death says essentially all that needs to be said, then the language used to describe the Gospel becomes, in effect, all that people in this frame of mind care about.

In light of conventional teaching on the atonement, then, I can feel *relief* for this changed status. I get to avoid eternal separation from God. I can therefore even feel *grateful* for what God has done *for me*. But if, over the course of time, I do not encounter any other teachings to help fill out and develop my understanding of the nature and purposes of God; if I experience a dearth of more comprehensive teaching on this point; if, furthermore, I follow the normal course of things and begin to think of doctrine as primarily about intellectual boundary matters, my initial faith in Christ remains pitifully underdeveloped; maybe even dies aborning.

Again, so as not to be misunderstood, I fully acknowledge the absolute centrality of a personal, dispositional, trusting, humble, penitent relationship with God. At the risk of too much repetition, I am therefore not criticizing the penal substitutionary theory of the atonement. It forms a necessary part of our faith. I am, on the other hand, strongly criticizing the way popular teaching about Jesus' death virtually makes a caricature of the significance of Jesus' death, precisely because we do not connect it with other critical doctrinal teaching points. This lack has resulted in the church's almost completely losing sight of the sanctifying work of God subsequent to being justified by faith.

The most popular versions of American Christianity place almost exclusive emphasis on the first step of the Christian life, inviting people across that threshold of *justification*. There has not been a corresponding emphasis on *sanctification*, on growing Christian disciples who individually and collectively embody and make visible the purposes of a loving, merciful, yet *holy* God. I realize that you can find any number of laudable efforts aimed precisely at Christian formation, yet, if you think about the general impact of this boiled-down doctrine that I am criticizing, my point stands. The attention given to what God has done *for us* in Christ is crucial and not to be minimized, yet in order to exhibit growing, fruitful lives, we must also think again about what God, through the Holy Spirit, is doing *in us*. We have not found a way adequately to address this challenge.

The formative impact of doctrine, i.e., that doctrine not only teaches us what to think about but also what to care about, in today's Christian climate gets short shrift to the detriment of our lives. This oversight has resulted in an unbalanced focus on external matters, on our status with

God, and has left largely unexamined the internal, heart-related concerns that deal with thoughts, feelings, dispositions, and actions. It leads straight to another slogan I have criticized: Christians aren't perfect, just forgiven. Paraphrasing John Wesley, we know that Jesus has saved us from Hell. We do not see that Jesus came also to save us from sin.

Imagine what might happen to the quality of both our spiritual lives and our witness, therefore, if more of us undertook the work of engaging doctrine more comprehensively and persistently. The "content of our character," to quote Dr. Martin Luther King, would shine with the glow of Jesus' holiness and compassion. And the quality of our Christian community and our witness would follow. You see? Doctrine is, in the end, very practical!

QUESTIONS AND OBJECTIONS

Clearly, I have been covering complex and deeply important matters of concern. Intelligent, godly thinkers have been studying and debating this material since the beginning of the church. I am keenly aware of the shallow and even anemic way I have handled these subjects. I can therefore imagine certain questions and objections, so let me try to answer them.

Immediately a common objection regarding doctrine comes to mind. Does getting an idea wrong mean that a person's spiritual life will suffer? Is one's spiritual life going to tank simply because one does not have every concept intellectually worked through and every problem resolved? What kind of God would make the quality of one's spiritual life, and perhaps even one's eternal destiny, hang on doctrinal correctness?

This is a common objection and it challenges us to ask some good questions. How do we allow for the inherently limited nature of human reasoning about God? Can not and does not God work in spite of our limitations? In other words, couldn't someone really love God authentically and adequately while having less-than-adequate concepts of God? Well, yes, and no.

The biases about doctrine that I am criticizing—that one's specific beliefs do not matter much so long as we love God—actually hide a more basic claim, which, when exposed to the light, is clearly absurd. That claim is that doctrines ultimately do not matter as long as one loves God. To love God means that we need to believe that we actually know something about the Being to which we have assigned the term "God." We find ourselves immediately confronted with a doctrinal concern. Furthermore, even the injunction to love is based on an already assumed doctrine, that God is by nature loving and that we love in response. Again, doctrine.

Therefore, while it is certainly true that we can and most certainly do possess incorrect ideas about God or the Christian life and still have a wonderful relationship with God, it is also true that lots of wrong ideas accumulating over time, especially about important matters, will have a progressively weakening effect than fewer wrong ideas would have. Obviously, it is better to be closer to the truth than farther away. If doctrine teaches us what to care about as well as what to think, and if, furthermore, *thinking* and *caring about* actually belong to the same mental process, then we have all the more motivation to pursue sound doctrine.

Now let me get to another objection often raised in relation to calls to pay more attention to doctrine, like the one I have advanced here. It is a point that disturbs some of my friends and colleagues who get nervous when I start talking about doctrine. Here I circle back to a point I made earlier that expresses anxiety about the use (abuse, rather) of power in relation to doctrine. They speak to a concern that we all must hear and to which I am very sympathetic, for it is very important for the unity of the Body of Christ. Doctrine should never be used as a weapon to exclude or estrange people. Doctrine has power, but it is not a tool to dominate and control. I want to speak very clearly here: my motive for upholding the critical importance of sound doctrine is not simplistically to figure out "who's right and who's wrong." On the contrary, sound doctrine bears the peaceful fruit of righteousness. It matters for human flourishing.

Thus, in emphasizing the powerful influence of doctrine, I have no interest in its use for excluding people. Certainly, for any group to be identified as such, it must have conceptual boundaries of some kind. Otherwise, who could identify it as a group? Inevitably, thinking about doctrine raises questions about the degree to which one must agree and conform in order to identify with a group, so implications of inclusion and exclusion must arise. But this is not a challenge that Christians concerned with doctrine must face. Every group of any kind faces the exact same challenge.

Finally, while these sorts of questions and concerns are important and demand thoughtful response, they quickly recede in importance in light of the ignorance and less-than-fruitful witness of the church in today's world. If doctrine does in fact what I have argued that it does, then doctrinal ignorance has led inevitably to the church's poor witness as well as poor thinking. We do not adequately understand that doctrine shapes our dispositions and what we care about as well as what we think. The concern that doctrine leads to a church guilty of exclusiveness reveals more about our culture's assumptions about power than it does about doctrine, by its claim that the main use of doctrine is to dominate and control.[25] I have no interest in such a use. Rather, I want to turn the notion on its head. Rather than manipulating doctrines in order to control others, we in some sense *give up control* and yield to the Spirit's formative work through doctrine.

First Timothy 4:6 thus describes doctrine in a manner more in keeping with my aim in this chapter: "If you put these instructions before the brothers and sisters, you will be a good servant of Christ Jesus, *nourished on* the words of the faith and of the sound teaching that you have followed" (emphasis added). Nourishment gives and sustains life. The teaching to which this verse refers nourishes and sustains the life we have in Christ. The Greek word for *nourished* in this verse, *entrephomenos,* suggests the continuously life-giving function of doctrine. This is exactly what doctrine is supposed to do; it so permeates our whole being that we are entirely shaped by it. It imbues and nourishes us, whole people, every part of our thinking, feeling, and acting.

Our lack of systematic engagement with doctrine has rendered perhaps the most disheartening consequence with regard to our view of the church. Many forces—historical, political, and intellectual—contribute to this sad situation. An individualistic approach to the Christian faith that characterizes evangelical Protestantism in North America keeps questions about the church on the sideline, while erstwhile mainline denominations have been struggling with denominational decline. In either case, the Church's profile in American public life has been both shrinking and worsening in terms of popular opinion. It is definitely worth our paying attention to this most important topic.

Can a whole congregation exhibit the qualities of Christ-likeness that I have been pointing to as spiritual maturity? Yes. With humility born from recognizing the tenacity of sin, we nonetheless must face the Bible's call for the whole church to commit to growth to maturity. It is a matter not only of the well-being of Christ's Body. Maturity is a matter of mission.

25. James Davison Hunter has written very perceptively about this matter in his recent book, *To Change the World*.

6 Maturity and Mission
The Corporate Dimension

> Love cannot be hid any more than light; and least of all when it shines forth in action, when ye exercise yourselves in the labour of love, in beneficence of every kind. As well may men think to hide a city as to hide a Christian.[1]

THE USUAL WAY WE THINK OF "CHURCH"

Imagine being part of a group of believers like the one mentioned in 1 Thess 2:6–7: "And you became imitators of us and of the Lord, for in spite of persecution you received the word with joy inspired by the Holy Spirit, so that you became an example to all the believers in Macedonia and Achaia." Notice the following points:

1. They imitated Paul and his team, who themselves were imitating Christ. Does it seem ridiculous to think that church members could emulate their leaders?

2. In hearing and receiving God's Word, they joyfully demonstrated God's power in such a manner that the whole community of believers was recognized for faithful witness.

3. In spite of persecution (maybe because of it?), their life bore fruit. People could see the vibrancy and winsome quality of their faith.

---

1. Wesley, "Sermon on the Mount, IV," in *The Works of John Wesley*, 1:539.

Consider also Paul's exhortation to the Philippians (2:5): "Let the same mind be in you [second person plural] that was in Christ Jesus." Can we imagine a community of believers sharing the mind of Christ? The word *mind* trips us up because of the strong connotation with "intellect" or "opinion." It does not mean that Paul intended the Philippians all to think exactly the same way about every matter (impossible, not to mention exceedingly undesirable). We will see shortly that "mind" does not refer only to intellect, but also to disposition. The "mind of Christ" is reflected, in this christological hymn, also in his willingness to humble himself in compassion and obedience, for the sake of his mission. The Philippians were called not only to show unity around common beliefs, but were also to commit to one another in humility and self-sacrifice, just as our Lord was so committed.

Snapshots like these from the New Testament prompt the question: can a group demonstrate spiritual maturity? Can a whole congregation reveal the mind of Christ? It stretches the imagination to think this way. Certainly, spiritual maturity exhibited by a group will always be fluid and changing, because the makeup of groups changes regularly through people's joining and leaving. Once again we come face to face with a compelling biblical principle that has slipped from our awareness. We are empowered by the Spirit of God collectively to grow to maturity *precisely for* the sake of God's mission. The call to grow to maturity is inseparable from the call to minister. Living the Christian life not only gets you and me into heaven. It puts us to work in God's kingdom.

Because of the individualistic attitudes dominant in our culture, we have to work a bit harder to see what the Bible has to say about the group dimension of the Christian life. For example, in the Phil 2 passage to which we just alluded, the clause "Let the same mind be in you . . ." translates essentially one Greek verb, *phroneite*, which is a second person plural form. We typically think of "mind" as an individual person's private thoughts. Even so, when a matter is important to a group, they can search for "being of one mind," which means that they not only find some level of agreement but also, more importantly, some common course of action. *Phroneite* as a second person plural verb thus points to *shared* concerns, ideas, and commitments. The term leads us, therefore, to think of the importance and quality of relationships within a community. The closer we get as a group to having the mind of Christ, to demonstrating the powerful, humble, world-changing love of Christ, the more mature we become as a group.

You may be aware of the strong negative impressions that many people have about "organized Christianity."[2] It is sad to realize that many of the negative opinions about church come from people who have firsthand experience with Christians. They have tried participating in Christian communities. They have given the Church a real chance and have left disillusioned and, worse, wounded. They may still admire Jesus, but they have felt judged and turned away by people who profess to follow Jesus. It does us no good to feel defensive and start rationalizing. Whether the harsh criticism accurately reflects the situation or not, we must face squarely the negative public opinion and do some collective soul searching. I have witnessed enough anguish especially among young people about the church to be convinced that we need to repent and make changes.

To be sure, even in the New Testament age, Jesus' followers had their struggles. Reading through 1 and 2 Corinthians, for example, we see the conflict and strife present in Corinth. Even among the disputants whom Paul criticized, however, he found qualities that clearly point to the visible work of God: "I give thanks . . . for you because of the grace of God that has been given you in Christ Jesus, for in every way you have been enriched in him, in speech and knowledge of every kind . . . so that you are not lacking any spiritual gift" (1 Cor 1:4–7). Early Christians faced all kinds of problems, yet also demonstrated a quality of relationships that exuded confidence in Christ, joy, and extravagant generosity that people outside the church and throughout the region noticed.

The evidence for the truth of what the Scriptures say about exemplary churches can be seen in how the church grew from apostolic days to the time that Emperor Constantine converted to Christianity in the early 300s and gave the faith legal standing. Some years ago Rodney Stark wrote an interesting, if somewhat conjectural, study of how the early church grew. Using the research methods of modern social science, Stark took

---

2. Consider these recent books: Kinnaman and Lyons, *UnChristian*; Kimball, *They Like Jesus but Not the Church*. You likely have heard of the so-called Emergent Church books by Tony Jones (*The New Christians*) or Doug Pagitt (*Church Re-Imagined*). I could name many, many more. Whether one agrees with all the claims made in these books, their very existence and number illustrate the unhappiness that many people feel with the quality of the church's collective witness.

the most useful data he could find on the number of Christians present in the Empire,[3] and pieced together a picture, covering about a 350-year period, of how the church grew. One characteristic stands out: the faithful, sacrificial witness of the Christians to their neighbors. One particularly intriguing chapter in the book, "Epidemics, Networks and Conversion," shows this courageous and compassionate witness. During times of plague and pestilence, while wealthy pagans could and did flee to their country villas, Christians stayed and nursed the sick and dying, pagan or Christian, risking their lives in service to others. This sacrificial ministry made the Christian faith attractive to pagan neighbors, and it opened a door for Christian apologists to speak to the intellectual strength of the faith as well.[4]

This feature of exemplary and effective witness that Stark has sought to quantify, church historians have written about for years. For example, pondering the amazing growth of the Christian faith in the early centuries, Kenneth Scott Latourette has written, "In the five centuries after the death and resurrection of Jesus, the religion which had him as its centre took form, won the professed allegiance of the large majority of the peoples of the Roman Empire, and spilled over beyond the boundaries of that realm. Here is one of the most surprising developments of history."[5] Similarly, Latourette quotes Professor T. R. Glover, of Cambridge University, "Christians out-thought, out-lived, and out-died the adherents of the non-Christian religions."[6] This reputation of the church was forged in the fires of a pagan majority culture that, at times, badly misunderstood the theology and practices of the Christian faith.[7] Are most of our congregations in today's generation known for such qualities? Do we consistently demonstrate these values?

3. One source for numbers of Christians from the earliest times comes from the historian Eusebius, Bishop of Caesarea, who wrote *Ecclesiastical History* during the time of the Emperor Constantine. Eusebius is known as the "father of church history."

4. Stark, *Rise of Christianity*. See especially pps. 73–94 for material on the chapter noted above.

5. Latourette, *Christianity through the Ages*, 31.

6. Ibid.

7. One example of the ignorance: Christians were sometimes accused of cannibalism because of the Lord's Supper, in which believers consume the body and blood of Christ. It is simple to see how this confusion crept into popular consciousness.

SOME TECHNICAL TERMS AS TOOLS FOR THINKING

To understand the corporate dimension of spiritual maturity, we need to think about the deep connections between the qualities of individual discipleship that we have examined thus far and their application to communal relationships and activities. In order to do so adequately, I must introduce other technical theological terms to go along with our use of Christology in the previous chapters. Those terms are soteriology (doctrine of the Christian life or salvation), ecclesiology (doctrine of the church) and eschatology (doctrine of last things). As I have attempted to do throughout this book, I want the reader to have access to concepts that scholars regularly use, but which do not translate to normal, ordinary language among Christians. Dealing with ideas related to these terms is a necessary preliminary step in the work of this chapter.

The first term, soteriology, covers the Christian life as a whole, not just the initial moment of justification. It relates directly to the goal of sanctification mentioned in the previous chapter. In popular references to the Christian life, unfortunately, the concept of salvation often gets reduced to the moment of conversion. In this vein, people tend to think of "being saved" as a status—one is in right relationship to God and is thereby guaranteed a place in heaven. This view unwittingly weakens stress on the necessity of the commitment to daily growth this side of heaven. If being saved has to do primarily with the means to secure heaven, then, although Christians widely acknowledge the need for growth, the purpose of that growth, particularly in relation to communal and missional aspects of the faith, can be almost completely ignored. Ministry becomes one more option among many that we have to figure out how to fit into our busy lives.

In contrast to the common understanding of being saved, soteriology covers the whole of the Christian life. At the beginning of his essay "A Farther Appeal to Men of Reason and Religion," John Wesley wrote, "By salvation, I mean, not barely (according to the vulgar notion) deliverance from hell, or going to heaven, but a present deliverance from sin, a restoration of the soul to its primitive health . . . the renewal of our souls after the image of God in righteousness, true holiness, in justice, mercy and truth."[8] Soteriology thus covers the growth and development of the

---

8. Wesley, "A Farther Appeal to Men of Reason and Religion," Part I, in *The Works of John Wesley*, 11:106.

soul in Christ, which goes beyond conventional terms associated with Christian spirituality. Practicing usage of the technical term stimulates, one hopes, fruitful thinking about the whole of sanctified life.

Talk about "deliverance from sin" can make some readers nervous because it raises the specter of perfectionism. However, Wesley did not consider deliverance from sin to mean flawless perfection, and it is not necessary for us to agree on the limits of the concept "deliverance from sin" in order to work productively with what he is saying about salvation. It matters that we not get diverted by doctrinal controversy, but rather to stay focused on the Bible's call for growth in (and toward) holiness. Let us keep pressing on toward the heavenly calling, as Paul says in Phil 3.

This view of the individual Christian life (soteriology) has direct bearing on the doctrine of the church (ecclesiology). Questions about the determinative features of the church and how to recognize the true church have engaged theologians for many years. Two major descriptions find wide agreement across otherwise diverse groups. First, the church is one, holy, catholic, and apostolic. Oneness speaks to the church's unity and holiness to the peculiar relationship the church has with the triune God. The church as catholic speaks to its universal nature, which circles back to the notion of unity. Finally, the church as apostolic harkens to its foundations in the testimony of the apostles, which, in turn, relates to the New Testament documents. "Apostolic" can have the ring of "biblical," as well as referring to foundational authority of the original apostles.

The fourfold description of one, holy, catholic, and apostolic, gives a broad, global perspective of the church and raises numerous questions. Does unity require that all Christians belong to the same institution? Is unity rooted in beliefs? Is unity something spiritual without being institutional? Is the church holy by virtue of its status with God and its mission, or does the word mean something more moral, even ontological? Does apostolic mean an identifiable chain back to the original apostles through bishops or does apostolic mean "scriptural"?

One can ask about the nature of the church from the other side: what qualities absolutely, irreducibly, must be in place in order for the church to be visible? One standard answer to this question comes from the Protestant Reformation: the church exists where the pure Word of God is preached and the Sacraments duly administered. But here, too, we find questions. What constitutes the preaching of the "pure" Word of God? What about churches that don't think of the sacraments as sacraments but think of them as ordinances? This question relates directly to differing opinions about how God makes sanctifying grace available through practices like baptism and holy communion, but also through Scripture reading, worship, prayer, and the like.

Such questions have contributed to the proliferation of denominations and so-called nondenominational churches.[9] They are important, for they deal with what we could call boundary matters.[10] Yet, framed in this way, such questions remain somewhat distant from attitudes and dispositions associated with the life of salvation. We can become so preoccupied with group identity and boundary questions that we fail to grow in other ways and, worse, do not engage in the mission to which God calls us.

Consequentially, we mistakenly keep conversations about the Christian life and the church separate from one another. This tendency contributes not only to fragmentation among groups, but also within groups. It is not uncommon to find believers in a congregation working to grow spiritually through the practice of individual spiritual disciplines while engaging in church disputes in ways completely disconnected from the attitudes that should be fostered by their efforts at individual spiritual growth. Ironically, while people give attention to soteriology (the Christian life), they do not see its direct link to ecclesiology (the nature and purpose of the church).

What if we also thought of what it might mean, for example, to understand our being restored to the full image of God (Eph 4:24), in communal terms; if we thought of "image of God" also in relational terms? Consider the description of the image of God in Genesis 1 and 2. We learn there that being created in God's image means basically that human beings "look like" God in terms of rationality, morality, and politics. They have the ability to think, to communicate, to imagine, plan, build, and organize. In Genesis 2, we learn that human beings are designed *for each other* as well as for God. We too narrowly read the text on Adam and Eve as having to do with marriage. It does, of course, but it also speaks about human society as a whole. Human beings are created for relationship,

9. Even "nondenominational" churches have doctrinal orientations that place them within certain theological traditions, whether they officially belong to a denomination or not.

10. Over the centuries, we have spent much time and ink (not to mention blood) arguing about boundary matters.

for community. Thus, when the Spirit of God works on us to restore the image of God in us, it means that the nature of our communities should begin to look like God. "Image of God" has a corporate dimension that we too often overlook, much to the detriment of our life together. The term "ecclesiology," therefore, has much more work to do than simply to establish the characteristics of an authentic church.

When we add eschatology to the other two "-ologies," at first glance we seem to be adding an entirely unnecessary category, but, in fact, this is not the case. Eschatology deals with "last things," exploring questions of human destiny: the intermediate state,[11] heaven, hell, the new creation, the restoration of all things. It includes discussion about in what manner Christ will return (spiritually? literally?) to establish his Kingdom on earth. With regard to this subject matter probably more than any other in the Christian faith, we have been taught by popular books and movies. A generation or two ago, many of us devoured Hal Lindsey's best-selling *The Late Great Planet Earth* with much (often morbid) fascination. The very popular *Left Behind* series has taught people to think about biblical prophecy and the end times within certain categories that, in truth, come from but one of several legitimate systems of thinking about end times.[12]

The terms we often see in relation to eschatology obscure a very important point: "biblical prophecy" and "end times" language have within them an *operative view of history*, or, to say it another way, a working theory about history. Hence, when writers discuss end times prophecies they make all sorts of claims about how we should understand past and present history,[13] but we readers do not necessarily adequately recognize this point, even though we easily see the references to various geopolitical conflicts that are daily part of the news. Always, while discussing the future (end times), we should think about history. Ironically, people who don't like history can be enthralled by biblical prophecy and end times

11. "The intermediate state" refers to that period between an individual person's death and the ultimate end of time. Paul deals with this question in 1 Thess 4 because Christians were concerned about what happened to their brothers and sisters who died "in the Lord," but before the Lord's return.

12. For a very helpful survey of the different views of the end times, see Grenz, *The Millennial Maze*.

13. See, for example, Hagee, *Jerusalem Countdown*. Hagee clearly has a view of history at work that goes beyond what a term like "end times prophecies" would suggest. I strongly disagree with his analysis, but I recognize that he has a view of history that many Christians share.

writings even though it is impossible to separate the two. Considering eschatology means that we think about what God is doing throughout history and, by extension, the church's place in history.

I wish, therefore, to take up an aspect of eschatology that, because of our popular fascination with end times, goes under-examined. Eschatology also has to do with *ends* in the sense of God's final *aims* or ultimate *purposes*; God's will in the ultimate sense. While students of endtimes prophecy may acknowledge this point, their attention (and that given by the media) remains fixed narrowly on what will happen at the end of time.

To shift the focus, we ask what may seem like an odd and unanswerable question, How is the future invading the present? The philosopher Hannah Arendt describes the human will as that part of the mind oriented toward the future (especially in terms of desire), like memory is the mind oriented toward the past.[14] A big part of our mental life is given toward imagining our aims for the future. If I want to realize a certain future desire, (say, finishing a degree), then I must act *now* in ways that keep the goal fixed and operative in my mind. My future aim thus at least partially governs how I act in the present. In that sense, the future is guiding or "invading" the present. Theologically (in big picture terms), then, the future "invading" the present has to do with the final, ultimate will, desire or aim of God—which we experience as future, as yet to be realized—unfolding in the present through God's actions. If we think of God working in this way, then the question, How are God's ultimate purposes working out in history now? takes on new significance. It does not negate interest in end times but it does focus on matters that involve us more directly *now*, in these days.

The links with the other two theological categories, the doctrine of salvation (soteriology) and the doctrine of the church (ecclesiology), now come more adequately into view because the nature and expression of both individual discipleship (salvation) and the collective expression of our faith as communities of followers of Jesus (the church, ecclesiology) can be seen as directly connected to God's final purposes (eschatology). In short, our individual lives as followers of Jesus, coupled with our communal life as a Body of Christ, bear witness to the fullness of God's redemptive plan for the world. This view takes us far beyond the common

14. Arendt, *The Life of the Mind*. See within this volume, "The Philosophers and the Will," 13.

feeling of obligation that individual believers have "to witness." While we seek to express faith in Christ individually, we also inevitably express it relationally and communally as well. It matters, therefore, how we live as followers (individually and communally) of Jesus now. God's (eschatological) aim for the destiny of the nations thus necessarily governs both individual relationships with God *and* the mission of the church.

This set of assumptions helps us consider some extremely important questions. For starters, how does one's individual life help fulfill God's purposes in the world? We should not be intimidated by such a question, nor put it out of mind as too idealistic, therefore irrelevant. It leads to a second question: how does the church both witness to the reality and work toward the realization of God's redemptive purposes? In other words, how do we individually and collectively embody and witness to the Kingdom of God as described in the Bible? How do the individual and the communal both contribute to effective mission?

All three technical terms that I have introduced—soteriology, ecclesiology, and eschatology—point to a vision of Christian maturity that, although clearly written in the biblical record, hardly sees the light of day in our everyday thinking. I invite you to consider this biblical challenge and to examine your commitments in its light. Because we are dealing with the broad sweep of history, we will break our pattern of scriptural investigation, which, thus far, has considered only New Testament passages. For this work, we must start with the Old Testament.

OLD TESTAMENT STARTING POINT

Let us start this part of our task by attempting to read the Ten Commandments through a different set of lenses than commonly used. Because of United States political and religious history, the Ten Commandments have been held in high esteem, while their purpose is little understood in biblical context. The common "civil religion" reading of the Ten Commandments takes them away from their missional purpose and puts them to work for a somewhat alien aim. In this modern context, people (religious or not) typically refer to these commands (and the so-called golden rule from Jesus) as a way of measuring individual moral goodness and then, on this basis, of laying claim to God's blessing. Let's put these notions aside and consider how the commandments actually show us our identity and mission as part of the people of God.

Israel's exodus from Egypt provides the context for the Ten Commandments. Israel's actual departure from Egypt starts in Exodus 12, following the tenth plague. The Egyptians have urged the Israelites to leave: they've had enough of problems associated with this slave race. God's people have departed and have gone through the Red Sea crossing. After traveling through the wilderness, they arrive at Horeb/Sinai, the mountain of God, where Moses had received his original vision to be God's agent on behalf of Israel. I have long pictured Moses going back to that same mountain feeling desperate for another divine word. It's as if Moses is pleading, "OK, God, I got them out here, now what do I do with them?"

With Moses back on the mountain, then, God speaks a word that orients everything that will follow in the Old Testament. In Exod 19:5–6, God says, "Now, therefore, if you obey my voice and keep my covenant, you shall be my treasured possession out of all the peoples. Indeed, the whole earth is mine, *but you shall be for me a priestly kingdom and a holy nation*" (emphasis added). Notice the focus on the kind of community that God intends to form. Jewish Bible scholar Nahum Sarna has written, "This concept of priesthood provides the model for *Israel's self-image* and for its role *among the nations* of the world" (emphasis added).[15] Here we have it: identity and mission. Numerous scholars have commented on how surprising and unprecedented such a view is.[16]

Think about the bidirectional ministry of a priest. A priest represents (mediates) God to people and people to God. It takes a certain kind of person to engage in this ministry. More to our corporate vision in this chapter, however, we see in this text the Bible's claim for *the whole community* somehow to engage in this priestly ministry, to be that certain kind of people who help their neighbors see and come to know the true God. And, initially, the people of Israel accept this call. Exodus 19:8 captures their response. All the people, speaking as if with one voice, say, "All that the Lord has spoken, we will do." They thereby enter into covenant with God. They agree to be the kind of people that fulfills God's purposes.[17]

---

15. Sarna, *Exploring Exodus*, 131.

16. In *The Torah*, W. Gunther Plaut writes, "Ministering to the rest of humanity. This represented a unique idea: all the people and not merely a selected segment would have a special religious task" (2:204).

17. Bible scholar Walter Brueggemann explores the links between Exod 19:5–6 and other places in the Old Testament in which this feature of the covenant between God

Scholars have long noted that the Ten Commandments divide into two groups (hence the two tablets). The first set of commands organizes around the community's relationship with God. Thus, not having any other gods, sanctifying the Sabbath, and so on, aim at keeping the people—as a community—walking in relationship with God, which keeps them in touch with God's purposes. Honoring the Sabbath, therefore, is not merely a rule that God set up so that, by keeping it, we keep God happy. Honoring the Sabbath keeps God's people aware of who they are in relation to God by pointing them weekly to the very God who saved them. The second tablet organizes the way the people of God are to relate to each other. They are to tell the truth, especially in legal settings in which testimony is required. They are to avoid the bitterness and resentment that affects a community when people covet each other's goods (and spouses). Covetousness can lead to murder, and so on. By committing to embody these commands, God's people demonstrate the *kind of people* God is making of them.

If we keep this fundamental point in mind when we read the Ten Commandments, they read much differently than merely a list of moral injunctions. Think about how we Christians commonly treat them. Imagine the conversation one has with oneself when thinking of these commands: "You shall have no other gods before me." (Do I have any "spiritual" idols that get in my way of honoring God properly?) "Remember the Sabbath day, to keep it holy." (Do I take time off from work? Do I go to church?) "Do not take the Lord's name in vain." (Do I swear? Do I use foul language?) When we treat the Ten Commandments in this way, we turn them into nothing more than a means of measuring individual morality and, worse, we evaluate the quality of our spiritual lives on this basis. This approach quickly produces the assumption of merit, because we tend to assess ourselves positively. Yet if we look at the larger context, we start to see the kind of people God is creating and why being a certain kind of people is crucial for God's mission.[18]

---

and Israel is explored, for example, Gen 12:1–3 (the call of Abram) and Exod 49:6. See Brueggemann, *Theology of the Old Testament*, 430–34.

18. Again, as I have done elsewhere in this book, I do not so much want people to stop using the Ten Commandments to measure themselves individually as I want people to add to this practice the larger understanding of the kind of people we are to be together. We are to be the kind of people who communally accept and pursue God's mission.

Let me press: to understand the Ten Commandments in their proper framework, we need to attend to the difference between seeing them as a set of rules to govern individual behavior and ethical and legal foundation for a modern nation-state like the United States, on the one side, and the covenantal mandate of a missionary people on the other. We can, of course, read with benefit the Ten Commandments, as universal ethical principles. Reading them *only* this way, however, hides a crucial point for all who want to follow God's purposes. This is why I think it is necessary that we keep in mind the covenant agreement made between God and Israel in Exodus 19. We do not properly understand the Ten Commandments in chapter 20 if we ignore the "kingdom of priests and holy nation" of chapter 19.

This theme—Israel as a certain kind of people called to do God's work—permeates the whole Old Testament. First, we see from the beginning of the Exodus event itself that God "imbeds," so to speak, a sense of the people of God that extends beyond the notion of Israel as an ethnic entity. In the instructions given to the people to keep the Passover feast, we find this point in Exod 12:48: "If an alien who resides with you wants to celebrate the Passover to the Lord, all his males shall be circumcised; then he may draw near to celebrate it; *he shall be regarded as a native of the land*," (emphasis added). In other words, anyone willing to accept the covenant relationship with God and make his commitment to that covenant visible with the mark of the covenant (circumcision) would be welcomed as a full member of the community. Ethnicity, bloodline, place of origin: these qualities take second place compared to the primary relationship and covenant with God. *Anybody* willing to enter into this covenant is included.

We therefore do not adequately understand the mission of Jesus without having an adequate grasp of this Old Testament conviction, for Jesus' work grows organically from it. Most Christians have a basic understanding of Jesus' atoning work on the cross. Let us add (without taking away the central importance of the cross) to our perspective by looking at how Jesus' teaching shapes our understanding of the kind of people God wants us to become.

The Vision from Jesus' Teachings

Consider, for example, the Sermon on the Mount. I have picked it for two reasons. First, this sermon typically gets the same kind of moralistic treatment as the Ten Commandments. We easily reduce Jesus' teachings to rules, abstracted from any context, to measure individual righteousness. Even when we talk about them with respect to the Kingdom of God, the emphasis falls mostly on social ethics in a rather static way, rather than on the mission of God's people. Second, most scholars regard the Sermon on the Mount in Matthew as Jesus' authoritative interpretation of the Mosaic Law.[19] Therefore, we see the parallel between the Ten Commandments and Jesus' teaching. Like the Ten Commandments, Jesus' teachings reveal: (1) the kind of relationship we, as a people, are to have with God and (2) the kind of communal relationships we are to practice as the people of God. Significant for our work in this chapter, the Sermon also shows us Jesus' vision for the relationships of his disciples with people outside the covenant community. Clearly, Jesus' teachings take us beyond observance of a set of rules in order to prove that we are "good Christians."

Take Matt 5:13, "You are the salt of the earth." We tend to individualize the statement: "You (singular) are the salt of the earth," and then perhaps we think about the quality of our individual witness.[20] But the "you" in this verse is second person plural—"You [my followers, my disciples, collectively] are the salt of the earth." Thinking of the communal dimension of our witness does not negate the importance of individual witness. You (individually) are most certainly the salt of the earth. But think of the power of a whole community that recognizes they are supposed to be a certain kind of people committed to God's eternal administration (God's Kingdom).

Among the more difficult sayings of Jesus are his words about loving our enemies in Matt 5:43–48. Jesus simply cuts us no slack here. If we love only people who are like us—our religious tribe, our race, our socioeconomic rank—then we are no better than the hypocrites or the heathen. God's mercy is over all his works, including our enemies. God's rain falls on the righteous and the unrighteous. Then Jesus drives home the chal-

19. Although I am focusing on Matthew, the same points could be made from Luke 6–7, in which we find Luke's version of the sermon. In both cases (Matthew and Luke), we see that Jesus' teachings aim at forming a community of a *certain kind of people*.

20. I admit to the worry that many Christians in today's culture don't even think much about their individual witness.

lenge: "Be perfect, therefore, as your heavenly Father is perfect," (5:48).[21] Remember, with regard to "perfect" (Greek plural *teleioi*), Jesus does not offer some abstract universal moral value. Rather, he connects this injunction to the way we interact with our enemies. Loving enemies—inside or outside the community of faith—*shows* our maturity, our likeness to our Heavenly Father. Most importantly, exhibiting this disposition to love even enemies makes the Reign of God evident *in this world*. Loving enemies, therefore, does not reduce to a matter of "give peace a chance" or "can we all just get along." It goes far deeper. It takes the cruciform shape of Christ.

John Wesley took this particular teaching to heart as a measure of the legitimacy of his Aldersgate experience in 1738. In recounting what some people regard as his evangelical conversion, Wesley tested the authenticity of the change in his heart by thinking about Jesus' words regarding enemies. Wesley then wrote, "I began to pray with all my might for those who had in a more especial way despitefully used me and persecuted me."[22] He thus refers directly to the passage I just mentioned from Matthew 5, as well as to the beatitudes in the same chapter. Wesley believed—and I agree—that we can assess the quality of our faith by the manner in which we think about and treat our enemies.

And Wesley had enemies. In March 1738, two months prior to Aldersgate, he had begun preaching what he then called the "new doctrine" of justification by faith. In numerous congregations he upset hearers with this message because of its leveling influence in terms of social rank. It put every one, rich or poor, high or low, on the same plane before God's holy judgment, which upset some of the respectable church members. Wesley's journal entries indicate that several times in this two-month period he was barred ever from preaching in certain congregations again. Even before he had the assurance of his own salvation, Wesley made enemies and encountered difficulties in the itinerant ministry. I imagine that it was these persons and experiences he had in mind when, his heart strangely warmed with the love of Christ, he began to pray for his enemies.

One more example from the Sermon on the Mount: consider Jesus' words about entering the straight and narrow gate. How do we read these

---

21. For a more expansive description of this verse, see chapter 1.

22. "Journals and Diaries, I," in *The Works of John Wesley*, 18:250.

two verses in Matthew 7 and hold them together with, for example, Eph 2:8–9 ("For by grace you have been saved . . . and this is not your own doing")? Does not Jesus sound like a rigid and narrow moralist in Matt 7:13–14? How is the way to life narrow? How does walking that narrow way reveal God's Kingdom? How does it show the kind of people who are Jesus' mission-driven disciples?

To answer, consider the topics that take up most of this sermon. They generally have to do with a proper understanding and application of the Mosaic Law and of related religious practices (fasting, praying, etc.). Is it too much of a stretch to suggest that the broad and easy way that leads to destruction actually refers precisely to the way some of the religious leaders and other elites practiced the Law? Jesus criticized the religious elites' way of "following the Law," which, in practice, resulted in their using the Law for purposes that neutralized the Law's weightier concerns. This irony was not lost on Jesus: the Law turned against itself, as it were. We who are part of the "religious establishment" today need to consider how our interpretations of Scripture and our cultural practices might put us in the same situation with respect to Jesus' critique. In other words, Jesus aimed this word about the broad and narrow ways precisely at the people who thought it applied to others, as a warning to those who interpreted the Law so as to maintain outward, apparent righteousness while avoiding the Law's penetrating their hearts and changing their lives. He lambasted those who made a show of piety with their artificially disheveled appearance and fanfare, so that people would notice their "dedication."

It is a salutary exercise, therefore, to go through the Sermon on the Mount and think about specific teachings in light of what they say to us about the quality of our communities, about becoming a certain kind of people whose communal life reveals the love and mercy of God in Christ. Look at the topics Jesus covers: the Law and Prophets (they will be completely fulfilled); the harsh expressions of judgment that we level at people ("You fool!" Matt 5:22); adultery; divorce; oaths ("I swear . . ."); vindictiveness; love for enemies; acts of generosity (do we want public acclaim?); prayer; fasting; what we really treasure; our allegiances (two masters) and so on. Notice particularly Jesus' words about a tree and its fruit (it is known by what it produces, Matt 7:15–20), and think of the community as a whole rather than the fruit of individual believers. Think of hearing and doing the Word as a community rather than as an individual. Jesus' teachings describe the kind of people we are to be together in relation to God and with one another.

Taking Jesus' words this seriously seems like an unreachable goal. We are tempted, consequently, to drop our vision, to settle for less than what the Scriptures tell us. We are even tempted to use Scripture against Scripture, finding ways to soften the impact of Jesus' teaching. We find ways to rationalize our falling short of the goal. It goes something like this: We understand that Jesus is not demanding flawless performance. He is much too savvy about human struggle and sin. Besides, as God-incarnate, he is rich in mercy. So, since Jesus could not have been talking about perfect performance or even motives, we also should not be "perfectionists" about these matters.

As is so often the case with rationalizations, it is not the logic that causes problems. As soon as we start mentally down this path of subtly finding ways to soften Jesus' challenges, we begin to settle for less than Jesus commands. We feel the weight of the flesh. It's the age-old problem, but it is far better to stick with what Jesus says, recognize and confess openly our sin, and pray for grace to grow toward the vision than to downsize his teachings and give up on the call to fruitful witness.

With Jesus' teaching on the Kingdom as the backdrop for an adequate understanding of the kind of people God is creating, let us look elsewhere in Scripture for a similar theme. In a real way, all of the New Testament letters speak to this vision, but none is more bracing than the one found in the Letter to the Ephesians.

A VISION OF COLLECTIVE MATURITY: EPHESIANS

Ephesians contains a sweeping vision of history and the supremacy of Christ over all cosmic principalities and powers. Its insights reveal the deep relationship between the doctrines of salvation, the church and God's final purposes (soteriology, ecclesiology, and eschatology). It shows how the integration of individual Christian life with relationships in community actually makes visible God's glorious eschatological mission. Obviously we cannot do a whole commentary on this book, but select passages easily show us what we need to see.

Ephesians 1:8b–10 provides the starting point: "With all wisdom and insight he has made known to us the mystery of his will, according to his good pleasure that he set forth in Christ, as a plan for the fullness of time, to gather up all things in him, things in heaven and things on earth." Notice, first, the claim that God has *revealed* the mystery of his will. Human beings did not concoct this notion. It is not a matter of guesswork, even if we acknowledge both human limitation and outright sinfulness that potentially distort God's revelation. In the fullness of time, people responded to something God has initiated. Furthermore, "mystery" does not mean something to be solved by piecing together the clues in the correct way. Rather, it refers to something that we could not arrive at through the usual steps of human logic. This revelation originates in the mind of God and is *given* to the apostolic generation.[23]

Second, the verse points to an event that reveals "the fullness of time." Two Greek words, *pleroma* and *kairos*, call for some explanation. *Pleroma* means "fullness," but in more than a quantitative sense. To use a very trite example, I could fill my coffee cup to the very brim, so that, if I added even one more drop, it would spill over the edge. I then could talk about the fullness of the cup, but this analogy does not do full justice to the word *pleroma*. *Pleroma* cannot be measured in this way. *Ripeness* and *readiness* offer descriptive suggestions that help us grasp the *pleroma* of time, according to God's sovereign administration. *Pleroma* therefore points to a mysterious paradox: an event happens in history yet whose significance is not limited—in the way we normally think about history— to the merely human plane. Academic historians, by virtue of the limitations of their scholarly discipline, search for natural causes to explain events, but this event yields to no such rendering.

The fullness of time of which Eph 1:8–9 speaks transcends this limitation. It is truly cosmic in its scope. In fact, it comprehends history in a way that causes us to see all other historical events quite differently, and the Greek word *kairos* helps to make this point. It points to another dimension of time beyond *kronos* (i.e., chronology). *Kronos* measures time in sequence: seconds, minutes, hours, days, weeks, and so on. It gives us useful reference points so that we know where we stand in time. *Kairos*, on the other hand, refers to particularly momentous "times." The *kairos*

23. This claim about divine revelation raises a number of important questions. For example, how does an idea, as it were, that originates in God's mind translate to human minds? How do we get the idea that a particular idea came from God and not ourselves? Christians disagree as to the answers, a fact I want to acknowledge. The limitations of this book do no permit an attempt to resolve or clarify any of those difficulties.

moment is packed with significance, regardless of how long or short the chronology of the moment is. It mirrors the sense we get from *pleroma*.

In Ephesians, then, the phrase "fullness of time" applies to the whole impact of Christ's entering and thereby transforming history. The author of Ephesians thus makes the boldest of claims. In one brief proposition, he sets the framework for all of history. In using this very pregnant phrase, "in the fullness of time," Ephesians prepares us to attend to the nature and extent of Christ's Lordship *in the here and now*, even if we acknowledge our limited appropriation of this cosmic reality. In Christ, "in the fullness of time," God has established a heavenly plan (administration) made visible on earth. Again we turn to the Greek, because the choice of words gives important color to our understanding. The Greek word *oikonomian* translates literally into the English "economy." It derives from two Greek words: *oikos*, meaning "house" or "household" and *nomos*, meaning "law," "principle" or "ordering oversight." "Economy" thus means something like "household order" and can refer narrowly to one's own family affairs or to a much bigger scale, like the Kingdom of God. In this passage, it points to God's governing oversight of all of history. God's "economy" reveals the mystery of God's will. History fits within God's cosmic purposes.[24]

Ephesians thus proclaims that in Christ, God exercises world-changing power. And now, in Christ, "[God] has put all things under his feet and has made him head over all things for the church" (Eph 1:22). Note the allusion to Psalms 2 and 110, from which we get a picture of God exercising sovereignty over all nations through his Anointed One. As I noted above, we tend to spiritualize and individualize this claim. Of course we know that Christ is "spiritually" the Lord of all, but "spiritually" often can be something of a wiggle word in this context. We can agree that Christ is Lord, but we rarely consider how Christ exercises that lordship in the face of current events as they play out on our TV screens. We should take care, then, not even unintentionally to demean Christ's Lordship that is operative right now, in our day.

Which is precisely why the view of the church in Ephesians is so powerful and instructive for understanding Christian maturity: the church is the visible means whereby Christ demonstrates his power to change not just individual human lives, but whole groups of people—

---

24. My choice of words is tricky, because it raises questions about what God determines in advance. I simply want to acknowledge the question without pursuing this point in the text, because my concern lies elsewhere.

even whole societies—to form a radically new community, a new race, as it were. That a group of believers visibly demonstrates growth toward maturity is exceedingly important, even necessary, for this ultimate aim. The New Revised Standard Version wording of Eph 2:15 makes this point clear: "He has abolished the law with its commandments and ordinances, that he might create in himself *one new humanity* in place of the two, thus making peace." The more literal translation of the Greek, "*hena kainon anthropon,*" "one new man," seems to direct us toward the individual.[25] Looking at the context, however, one can see that Paul is still speaking in big-picture historical terms and, in fact, is talking about a concrete, historical reality: two groups of people who formerly lived in hostility toward one another but who are now joined into the same commonwealth, the Body of Christ. This staggering claim demands attention, because it has profound implications for our view of the church (ecclesiology).

As I noted in chapter 4 of this book where I discussed grace, long practice of Bible preaching has resulted in an overly individualistic reading of Eph 2. This fact reminds us of the importance of understanding how *our* historical context colors what we glean from certain Scriptures at certain times. Earlier in Eph 2 we read one of the classic Reformation texts for "grace alone": "For by grace you have been saved through faith, and this is not your own doing" (2:8). We commonly read the "you" there as an individual "you," when it is, in fact, the plural "you." Of course, this trust must be applied individually, so thinking of it in the singular is certainly legitimate. The problem comes in reading it in *exclusively individualized* terms. The "new man" in Christ in 2:15 is often thought of, then, in terms of how Christ has saved and is restoring the individual believer by grace.

But look at the context of Eph 2. Paul is still talking about God's administration, God's eternal oversight and purpose for human history, and Paul refers to two specific groups: Jews and Gentiles. Remember, the word *Gentiles* is the same as "nations." When we read "Gentiles," we understand that we are talking about all the nations who are not Jewish. "Gentile" is thus a shorthand term for "anyone who is not Jewish," any-

---

25. Which points out the challenge of translation. Sometimes the most strictly literal translation is not the most accurate in terms of transferring the original meaning to the new language. Bible translators refer to the concept of "dynamic equivalence"—finding the meaning in the original language and looking for a dynamic equivalent in the translated language, rather than literal word-for-word translations that might miss the point.

one not of "the people of God." And in Eph 2:13–14, we read that Christ has torn down the dividing wall of hostility between Jew and Gentile. In so doing, he has created (take note of this word) "one new humanity," a new, transformed community under the lordship of Christ. This is why Paul says at the end of chapter 2 that the Gentiles are now "citizens with the saints," that both Jewish and Gentile followers of Jesus are part of the same commonwealth. In a sense, a new nation, a new race, as I mentioned earlier, is being created in Christ.

One more important insight from the Greek text: Christ, in creating a new humanity, expresses exactly the same kind of divine action and power as we find in the original creation of the universe. The Greek term *ktisei* translates the clause, "that he might create." As Bible scholar Harold Hoehner notes, this verb always refers to God's special action of creation.[26] We find here an exceedingly important point: Paul envisions the church as a reality that spans the earth and the times, just as God's creating and redeeming power and oversight does the entire cosmos.

Notice likewise the eschatological (end times, ultimate divine purposes) character of these thoughts. The text is not speculating about what will happen at the end of time. It speaks to something that God *has already done* and is continuing *to put into effect in Christ and through the witness of the Body of Christ.* The church visibly demonstrates (proves) the lordship of Christ. We view the present age from the perspective of God's ultimate purposes yet to be finalized. This means that what is happening now and what will happen in the last days are powerfully integrated. Personal salvation (soteriology) ties to the church (ecclesiology), which serves God's ultimate purposes (eschatology).

In case the utter miracle of what Paul is telling us has not yet adequately sunk into our awareness, consider the people Paul addresses in Ephesians. Here we must look at the context again to see how dramatic this vision truly is. If you look at any standard introduction to the book of Ephesians, you will read about the city of Ephesus itself. It was famous for its political, economic, and religious prominence. It was the provincial capital for Asia Minor—political power. Because of its proximity to the sea, it was an important center of commerce. It claimed religious

26. Hoehner, *Ephesians*, 378.

prominence as well because of the presence of one of the world's Seven Wonders: the temple of Artemis (Diana), a fertility goddess.[27]

If you wanted to go, "where the action is," Ephesus would rank as one such place. Now consider Paul's claims. Whatever the people in the Ephesian halls of power and cultural influence thought they were doing, *God's action* (administration), which creates a new humanity and subdues all things under the Lordship of Christ, is being demonstrated *right now* in Christ's Body down the street, so to speak, from the halls of pagan power.[28] If you want to see the real action, don't look where people usually look. Look at this new community.

I think it almost impossible to overstate this vision of the comprehensive *oikonomian* of God, revealed and actuated in Christ's work and embodied in the church. It sets the framework for understanding the comments about growing to maturity in Christ found in Eph 4. It shapes how we read about spiritual gifts. It guides the way we think about the practical injunctions to husbands and wives, slaves and masters, parents and children in Eph 5. Paul's encouragement to live in a certain way was not merely for the sake of organizing this new community, but also in order that people who observed this new community could see Christ in them! For the sake of God's eschatological mission, we divergent, mixed-up, messy followers of Jesus learn to live and work together as the new humanity, and in our communal witness we reflect God's holy and saving purposes.

With this important background in place, we can begin to consider how *spiritual maturity ties explicitly to mission*. Growing together toward this aim as a group of believers prompts and shapes dispositions toward ministry to and with others.[29] This conviction guides our understanding of the spiritual gifts listed in Eph 4:11–13. Christ's gifts distributed in the Body have a certain aim. Christ gave some to be apostles, prophets, evangelists, and pastors/teachers for the sake of building up the Body of Christ, *so that all could become mature in Christ*. Individual soteriology

27. Remember the trouble Paul caused when he first visited Ephesus, because his evangelizing tampered with the temple economy. See Acts 19.

28. Some readers may feel concern that I sound like I am limiting God's action to just the church. I do not intend to give that impression.

29. As Paul states in 2 Cor 5:14, it is the love of Christ that "urges us on" or constrains us to engage in the ministry of reconciliation. Maturity in Christ brings a deepening love for God and for neighbor.

(the Christian life) gathers believers into a community of people committed to the same end—to maturity. Here we encounter the principle of the whole as greater than the sum of its parts. We are something together as a whole that we are not even as collectives.

This reminder we now apply to a corporate view of maturity: we envision it as fulfilling an intended purpose rather than achieving a certain condition or a *stasis* of flawlessness. Notice the standard of measure—the full stature of Christ. Christ gave us gifts so that the Body of Christ could look (and act) like him. When people look at us, they should be able to see him. It is not just about "me" and my personal growth to maturity. It is about "us" and our growth together, *for the sake of Christ's work.* This is as much the goal of maturity as is individual growth.

Christ calls his followers to engage in his ministry. This statement calls to mind Jesus' words to his disciples, "Very truly I tell you, the one who believes in me will also do the works that I do and, in fact, will do greater works than these, because I am going to the Father" (John 14:12).[30] And looking like Christ means not only doing the things that Jesus did, but also, in some sense, feeling the feelings that Jesus felt. Because the Spirit of God is at work in us through grace and because that same Spirit gives us gifts, we love God and neighbor the way Jesus told us to do. We love sacrificially, extravagantly, like Jesus, which means necessarily that we will begin to feel compassion toward those toward whom Christ feels compassion. This view speaks directly to the points I have made earlier regarding the emotional tonality of our thoughts and the dispositions to act which flow from both thought and emotion. We witness, by our love for one another and our peaceful (even if occasionally messy) relationships with our neighbors, that we belong to Jesus. In other words, what is truly in our hearts shows up in the way we live, just like Jesus said it would.

Taking together the explanations of the Sermon on the Mount and portions of Ephesians that we have covered above, and piecing it together with glimpses from other parts of Scripture, the picture clearly emerges of a community of followers committed wholeheartedly to living the way of Jesus. A mature church is a church captivated by the vision of a missionary God. Remember, such a quality comes only through the grace of God

---

30. I do not mean, with this point, to set up some unrealistic notion about how individual persons might have the power to heal or cast out demons or to have other supernatural gifts.

in the gift of Jesus Christ, in his atoning death and his powerful resurrection *and* in the presence of his Spirit in the community of disciples. It is all of grace. We know that we often fall short of the vision and that there are many complexities and challenges that require constant, humble vigilance. It will be no easy matter to strive to live as a community that consistently reflects the heart of Christ.

Nevertheless, we must keep in mind that being a certain kind of people—growing together toward the measure of the full stature of Christ—is not just for our own salvation, but for the world's. These teachings to the community are for the sake of mission, not just so that we can measure our internal (either individual or communal) holiness or standing with God. As important as those measures are, we also need to look at how keeping these covenant terms *equips us* for faithful, effective witness in the world. They do not merely give us a sense about our status with God, but also point to fitness for mission. Mission flows from the heart, the collective heart of the Body of Christ.

Let us hold ourselves accountable, therefore, to God's Word, for this vision. It brings to mind the prayer that Bob Pierce, the founder of World Vision, prayed, during his time as a missionary in Korea: "Let my heart break with the things that break the heart of God." Ponder the radical nature of this prayer. Consider how disorienting to our usual manageable religious life—making church membership fit a busy schedule—taking seriously such a prayer would be. More importantly, notice how much like Jesus, how reflective of God's heart this prayer is.

When I read these words from Pierce, I think to myself, "I want a heart like that." At the same time, I start to imagine the implications. Think about a whole group of people for whom praying a similar prayer represents the defining quality of their communal life. What if we shared a heart of this kind? What if, to return to Phil 2:5, we had the mind of Christ? We can have it! If (as Eph 4:24 indicates) we are together being renewed in the likeness of God, then together, as a body, through grace, God's character shapes our character. Our group disposition reflects God's missional purposes.

I hope that I have managed in some small way to provoke a readiness to aim for a mature church that fully embraces the call to embody the character and purposes of Christ. I have no illusions about our ability to realize such a vision, but admitting our limitations and confessing our sin in no way lessens the impact of Christ's call. Clearly, if we do not commit ourselves to corporate maturity, we will not realize it.

We need some criteria for assessment, therefore, so that we can check progress in growth. Assessment presents a difficult challenge, because we often depend on quantitative measures for evaluation and we are talking about qualitative things. When it comes to "practical application," it becomes far too easy to develop a simple, relatively manageable list of criteria for measurement. The problem with this common response is that it tends, by reification and abstraction, to disconnect biblical principles from relationship to God and others. Yet we must have some useful means for assessment. How are we doing on the path toward spiritual maturity? We will bring this study to a close with ideas to try in your personal life and in your group. The final chapter offers a framework for this task.

7 Assessment
How Are We Doing?

I began examining the classes, and every person . . .
*and by comparing what they were with what they are
now* we found more abundant cause to praise God.

—John Wesley, from a journal entry
dated November 5, 1747; emphasis added

THE CHALLENGE: EXPOSING CULTURAL ASSUMPTIONS

Now comes the task of finding useful criteria to help us move beyond the basics of the faith[1] into its deeper and more challenging dimensions. In this last chapter I will offer what I think we must include in any set of assessment criteria, but, at the outset, I want to note a dilemma. On the one hand, people need identifiable and useable measures in order to evaluate their spiritual lives. On the other, overprescribing such measures becomes counterproductive because it tempts us to lapse into list making. We make a list of do's and don'ts, then, rather than practicing a growing relationship with Christ in community with other Christians, we become fixated on measuring ourselves against the list. This form of assessment is too mechanical. It tempts us to think that if we can positively check items on it, then we're growing. Checking items on a list does not necessarily lead to growth, yet we need *some* way to do the important

---

1. Remember Heb 6:1: "Therefore let us go on toward perfection, leaving behind the basic teaching about Christ, and not laying again the foundation."

work of evaluation. I will try in what follows to walk this fine line, but we need to recognize the traps into which we can easily fall.

The measures commonly used for assessment are influenced by deeply embedded cultural assumptions that affect us in at least two unhelpful ways. First, they guide us to think of spirituality in almost exclusively individualistic terms. Even though most active Christians belong to some sort of congregation, the quality of communal life as a whole lies a distant second to individual concerns.[2] Church leaders, by virtue of occupation or office, pay attention to certain aspects of communal life, to be sure, but they most often lean heavily on quantitative measures, the number of people participating in worship as primary. If a church is growing numerically, people generally see it as evidence of God's blessing. Since the Christian faith is by nature evangelistic, and since numbers represent real people, we should care about numbers. But we should not care *only* about numbers.[3]

At the individual level, we see a different, yet highly recognizable checklist for measuring spiritual health. Again, I acknowledge the importance of the practices on this checklist, and I will return to a version of it later, but if we lose sight of the goal toward which the checklist is a means, then we lose sight of the vision of spiritual maturity. We can draw the wrong conclusions from mere activity, like whether we have a personal devotion time, whether we belong to a Bible study[4] or other small group, whether our financial support for the church is acceptable, and maybe even whether to go on a mission trip or join some other service activity.

Our culture's obsession with experience-rich environments further complicates a Christian's ability to assess spiritual growth. I recently attended a luncheon in which the Vice President of the Texas Rangers

2. Even using a word like *church* creates problems these days. The house church movement is growing, for example. A significant number of people do not belong to what we commonly think of as a congregation in the traditional sense of that word.

3. Every pastor I know would agree with this point, but the truth is, church leaders are ultimately judged by the number of participants and programs and by the size of budgets. These are all quantitative measures.

4. Among college students, the term "Bible study" covers an increasingly (and surprisingly) wide range of activities. Students often do not study the Bible at all. It is fairly common for students in these "Bible studies" to have some kind of devotional thought leading to group discussion. At the end of the day, even in Bible studies, there seems to be little actual study of the Bible.

shared thoughts on the team's recent success.[5] Of course he talked about their win-loss record, but he consistently returned to the priority of creating the kind of experience fans desire. This means that the organization must pay attention to a myriad of off-the-field concerns, from the comfort of the seats to the merchandise, from the hot dogs and drinks to the quality of TV monitors. Fans should never have a dull moment while in the ballpark. It is not just the game. It is the *experience people have* at the game, whether the team wins or loses. When these assumptions drive the way we assess the quality of our Christian life, the *day-to-day* requirements of growth can start to look utterly stale and lifeless, yet we make a big mistake if we let them dictate what we look for in spiritual growth.

To grow effectively, we need to gain some distance from these popular assumptions. Remember, we do not consciously think about them. We see through them. They are already part of our mental framework. We therefore need a workable degree of self-awareness, which comes by practicing thinking about our thoughts, feelings and actions in relation to specific circumstances.[6] Thinking about these matters reveals the deep links between the dimensions of the heart that we so easily separate from each other. Gaining self awareness begins to show how the emotional responses we make to situations flow from what we care about, which, in turn, can point to which beliefs and doctrines exercise the most influence in our thinking.

Self-awareness is a spiritual skill, recognized by leaders and experts in fields going far beyond the scope of this book. It is worthwhile for Christians to consider the significance of the number of books addressing this concern in a non-religious way.[7] It points to the need in public life,

---

5. The Texas Rangers are a Major League baseball team that went to the World Series in 2010. Winning the American League title was their first and marks a major turnaround of this organization in a short time.

6. The Puritans of the sixteenth and seventeenth centuries, followed by the evangelicals of the eighteenth and nineteenth centuries, have much to teach us in this regard.

7. In fact, the connection is so strong that *The Leadership Challenge*, by James M. Kouzes and Barry Z. Posner, has a companion volume, *Christian Reflections on the Leadership Challenge*. I have mentioned elsewhere *Emotional Intelligence*, by Daniel Goleman. In this same vein, see also Boyatzis and McKee, *Resonant Leadership*. Notice the emotionally tonal language of the title, as well as its overtly spiritual terms, probably employing Buddhist assumptions. See also Covey, *The Speed of Trust*; Patterson, Grenny, McMillan, and Switzler, *Crucial Conversations*. All these books deal explicitly with the challenge of developing self-awareness.

which means that followers of Jesus should take notice. This is our call! Self-awareness requires humility and openness of heart to accept what we find when we (and others) examine our hearts. In relation to practicing self-awareness, we will then also look at how doctrine and the disciplines or practices (from which we make the lists) are affected.

PROPER SELF-AWARENESS

Toward the end of *Primal Leadership,* Daniel Goleman and his co-authors discuss the problematic impact on organizations when leaders become insulated from co-workers and subordinates. The authors call it the CEO disease, "the information vacuum around a leader created when people withhold important (and usually unpleasant) information."[8] The result is a loss of self-awareness. The same problem permeates the church, affecting everyone across the board. On the whole, we are not very good at practicing this important task.

The main reason for the lack of self-awareness is that gaining it is often hard, *risky* work. I illustrate with an example from my own life. In my growing up years, I somehow mistakenly picked up the notion that being a "good witness" for Christ meant in effect acting as other people's conscience. I innocently but wrongly took it upon myself to point out when I thought people were wandering from God's way. I did not consciously think this practice through, of course. I just did it. You can imagine how well it worked, especially when I landed on the college campus and moved in to the fraternity house. One moment stands out as a painful (at the time) but valuable encounter with divine grace. God used it, difficult as it was, for my good.

One evening, a group of us college men gathered around the television[9] to watch the Miss America pageant. Even though college men generally love to look at beautiful women, they are not inclined to sit still for programs of this sort. It just so happened that I knew one of the contestants that year, so my buddies and I decided to watch. We gathered around the set in our TV lounge and settled in with snacks and drinks.

From the beginning of the program, my associates began peppering the room with catcalls, comments, and salacious groans at the images of

8. Goleman, Boyatzis, and McKee, *Primal Leadership,* 93.

9. For younger readers, this event took place before cable TV, and before everyone had a TV in his own room.

beautiful women on the screen. The comments quickly degenerated into the profane. Now comes my "witness." I began to chastise the men for their ribaldries. Before long, one of them swiveled in his chair, glaring, and exclaimed, "Well, I'm sorry, Holier-Than-Thou!"

I was stunned. He was absolutely right. I *was* holier-than-thou. Till that moment, I had no idea how disgustingly sanctimonious I sounded to people. The tricky part is that I really did care about these men. They were my friends, and I wanted each of them to have the kind of relationship with God that would make them morally sensitive, good young men. I wanted to help them avoid the corrosive effects of the coarse talk.[10] I wanted them to stay out of trouble with God.

This holier-than-thou moment became one of dawning self-awareness, hence of divine grace. God's Spirit took a word of truth, harsh as it was, and opened to me a vision of my own soul. It could have gone another direction. I could have shut down, emotionally. I could have defended myself, explaining that my friend had misunderstood my intention. I could have gone on the counterattack. In this moment, however, God intended to work on me, Joseph-like,[11] and I needed desperately not to squirm out from under the discipline. God was offering me the chance to see myself in a clearer light. This experience reveals how the heart works, the deep connections between what we think, what we care about and feel, and how we act. It speaks to material from chapter 2, where we explored how emotions help reveal what we think. So, let's walk back through the scene and look at what it teaches.

As the loose, risqué talk continued, I began to feel what could be called creeping moral alarm. The longer I listened, the more I felt concerned. (As an aside and to complicate the matter further, consider that I, as a young college man myself, enjoyed the "scenery" on the television screen every bit as much as my crude-talking friends. I was worried about myself as much as I was about them.) It prompted me to act, albeit in a not-so-helpful way, in part because of the limitation of my understanding. However, I did so not merely on the basis of a feeling. My concern traced back to my concepts of God's nature and will.

10. Because I knew one of the contestants, I could feel more easily the dehumanizing implications of the coarse talk. I also was thinking of Jesus' words about sexual lust.

11. I am here thinking of Joseph's comment to his brothers, "You meant it to me for evil, but God meant it for good." See Gen 50:19.

I understood that God is holy and does not countenance unholy behavior. I also knew that God is Judge, so my friends and I were answerable. Over time, teachings about God and the standards of a Christian life had worked their way into my consciousness, for good and ill, in this case. They significantly influenced what I *cared about*. I was responding most strongly to teaching on God's holiness and the divine right to judge our behavior. I therefore cared about staying in good stead with God and I wanted the same for my friends. In truth, I wanted us all to stay out of trouble with God. My beliefs, growing from doctrine, helped shape my dispositions, and my actions followed in suit. From a more mature view, I can see that, at the time, I lacked sufficient awareness of other aspects of God's nature, God's loving-kindness and patience, for example. I exhibited a basically fearful disposition, motivated to avoid God's wrath more than to share God's love. This basically fearful approach characterized my faith at the time.

This story shows that gaining self-awareness is both difficult and risky. One aspect of the "sin that clings so closely"[12] is our penchant for self-justification. We instinctively react to protect our sometimes very fragile egos. I think Christians (and probably Christian leaders) suffer this temptation more than maybe any other. We are masters at using Christian jargon to cover our tracks and explain away the impact of our behavior. That I needed help waking up to this weakness points to the power and necessity not only of self-awareness, but also of the role of community. We cannot grow to maturity on our own. John Wesley famously said, "No holiness but social holiness,"[13] by which he meant the necessity of community. Many people outside the Wesleyan tradition especially admire how Wesley insisted on Methodists participating in small groups. I think it is not unfair or inaccurate to say that, of all things Wesleyan, perhaps the small group ministries of many churches owe their existence in some sense to this legacy.[14]

12. See Heb 12:1.

13. Wesley, "Preface to 1739 Hymns and Sacred Poems," in *The Works of John Wesley*, Jackson edition, 14:321.

14. I suggest two sources to study for people interested in small groups in the Wesleyan tradition. Kevin M. Watson's *A Blueprint for Discipleship* expounds on the theoretical framework, so to speak, for small groups in a Wesleyan tradition. D. Michael Henderson's book, *A Model for Making Disciples*, gives the historical background to the class meeting (a central feature of the small group system in Methodism) and situates it within the whole system of groups that Wesley organized.

Gaining self-awareness is not always so painful. Sometimes it is downright exciting. A significant number of disciples have discovered spiritual gifts or have experienced a call to some particular ministry[15] because other people helped them become aware of those gifts that they themselves had never recognized. Rather than correction, this moment happens through a word of affirmation. Again, God is at work in such moments. The light comes on in one's mind, and one's heart quickens to the significance of the moment. This, too, enhances self-awareness.

So, how do we gain self-awareness? In answer, we can see why so much weight has been placed on the "quiet time" or personal devotions that populates our lists of measurable Christian practices. Usually, the "quiet time" includes Bible reading of some sort, using a devotional guide or reading a portion of a book, and prayer. In prayer, most people spend most of their time making requests on behalf of others and for themselves. All these actions are quite appropriate, of course. Once again, I do not wish to take anything way, but to add the habit of effective introspection, to explore the connections between thoughts and feelings. Introspection helps us break the cycle of merely going through the motions of a spiritual practice. In this sense, introspection is a significant feature of prayer, along with praise, thanksgiving, intercession, and supplication. It requires *listening* not only to our own hearts but also to what God might be speaking. The habit of journal writing can help develop the skill of introspection. It calls for more than simply writing down the day's events or merely describing our feelings. When we do this kind of reflection, we analyze. We look for relationships and causes in our thoughts, feelings, and motives. We can discover qualities and patterns.[16]

So much more could be said regarding *individual* self-awareness, but hopefully I have offered enough for clarity of the idea. Let us turn now to the corporate dimension. How does a group practice self-awareness? Even asking the question perhaps seems slightly off. Can a group exhibit

15. I am using "ministry" here to cover all such activities, by lay or clergy. I hope more and more laypeople begin to realize that they are, in fact, engaged in ministry as they exercise their gifts.

16. In light of my "holier-than-thou" moment, I began to realize over time how much my experience of the Christian life was driven by fear. Many people, no doubt, would not be surprised by this discovery. However, we tend to use therapeutic terms for this discovery, rather than biblical or theological, since it has to do mostly with emotions. Therapeutic terms are certainly helpful, but they do little for helping us develop thoroughly Christian, therefore spiritually mature, dispositions.

self-awareness? Unfortunately, this question is easier answered by negative examples than positive. Consider mob psychology. A peaceful demonstration turns into a dangerous riot. What happened? It is hard to say, but something mysterious and chaotic emerges seemingly from nowhere and people are punching each other, hurling bottles and debris, and overturning cars. The people acted "as one," as if a single mind moved them.

Although it takes work, we can see a single mind moving a group for good, which is exactly what Paul had in mind in exhorting the Philippian believers to share the mind of Christ.[17] Given the need for peaceful relations in today's uncivil and coarsening society,[18] followers of Jesus have a singular opportunity to bear fruitful witness. Furthermore, when we consider the foundational truth of being created in God's image, we see (Gen 1:26–27; 2:18ff.) that we are created for community. Even modern neuroscience points to the same reality, thereby supporting the Bible's point.[19] A group can practice self-awareness a number of ways. Most of these suggestions are already well known. As I have said elsewhere in a number of places, our problem is not so much with specific activities as it is with the fact that we do not connect them to the goal of spiritual maturity, and the lack of vision undermines the effectiveness of the practice.

A congregation could start practicing self-awareness by discussing the purposes of all the church's programs in light of the trajectory toward maturity explained in chapter 3. And I do mean all programming. We will discover, of course, that the same ministry can speak to a diversity of locations on the trajectory. A Sunday school class, for example, normally includes people who are strong and growing Christians as well as people who are unsure and seeking. They might be awakened, to use the term from chapter 3, but not yet confident that they have fully entered the faith. If the goal is growth toward maturity, then what that class studies and how they relate to one another will likely look different than responding to whatever the current interests of the most vocal members might be.

17. Phil 2:5.

18. Road rage is a common reference in conversations these days. Other forms of uncivil and verbal (and sometimes physical) violence abound. I have been concerned for years about the increasingly cruel tone of reality TV shows such as *American Idol*, in which they basically make fun of people of lesser (or no) talent in the early stages of the season.

19. For a very readable explanation of the neuroscience underlying human sociality, see Goleman, *Social Intelligence*. See especially ch. 6, "What is Social Intelligence?" 82–104.

It is well worth a congregation's time, therefore, to ask questions in light of the trajectory. How does a congregation connect to people, for example, who might be asleep? Most often, it will do so through friendship and other networks. This suggestion means something other than what we normally imagine with evangelistic outreach, for example. I am talking about something much more basic. Imagine a congregation making a covenant to the effect, "We will act toward friends, neighbors, family members and co-workers in such a way that reflects the goodness and love of Christ. We will regularly check ourselves and we will ask our neighbors for feedback."

A congregation could follow through with asking a similar question about each part of the trajectory. "What ministries do we provide for people awakened to their need for God?" Churches need more than a membership class to address this need. Thinking about small groups, recovery programs, youth ministries, and college ministries, to suggest only a few, speaks to the needs of awakened people. The same question goes for new Christians and growing Christians. It means persistently asking questions about how programming connects to the goal of spiritual maturity. Churches need to find ways to practice asking questions about how all their programming aims at the goal.

Corporate self-awareness could also involve the use of surveys and other more formal opinion-gathering devices to learn what people outside the congregation think about that congregation. What is a congregation "known for"?

With regard to assessment, therefore, we start with asking ourselves—individually and collectively—how we are doing with self-awareness? What are we learning about ourselves? Are we open to other people's opinions (inside and outside the church) to help us gain self-awareness? Do we listen to the Spirit's teaching, correcting, comforting guidance? What would happen if we began to ask such questions persistently and systematically both for individual spiritual growth as well as for corporate growth?

TAKING DOCTRINE SERIOUSLY

Practicing self-awareness should generate a sense of both where we are strong and where we lack with regard to the theological content of the faith. We need to move away from the smorgasbord approach, driven by individual prerogatives and felt needs. The problem is not that we try to address felt needs. The problem is the *ad hoc* way we go at these concerns, allowing too much our whims and fancies to guide activities. Remember, with repeated exposure, what we read or listen to shapes what we care about and what we care about guides what we read. It also affects what we actually do. Doctrine helps form disposition, which, in turn, leads to action. Growing to maturity thus calls for a different approach to doctrine. The Christian life involves many topics and we should engage, over time, the whole range.

The basic categories associated with systematic theology provide help on doctrinal formation. Researchers of emerging adults have named doctrinal ignorance as one of the most pressing problems of our day. For the pragmatic reader who may feel tempted to turn away at this point (thinking that all this talk about theology is too academic and disconnected from real life), notice the practical outcome of lack of attention to doctrine. In spite of all the resources spent and all the activities invested in youth ministry, young people are entering adult life spiritually unprepared and confused by a cacophony of voices in a religiously diverse world.[20] Basic teaching across the categories of systematic theology is exceedingly important, therefore, especially in this period of time, and not only for young people. Longtime members of churches have gone tragically undernourished, which is one of the reasons our young people see only a surface level, compartmentalized faith in us.

Because the material of theology is so vast, we can be intimidated into inaction or avoidance, but there are resources that provide good basic introductions.[21] To use the well-known biblical metaphor, they will help us move from milk to meat. We need it for our *hearts*, not just our heads. If I sound like I am pleading, I am. To grow to maturity, people need exposure to the range of topics in systematic theology. If you already know what these terms mean and how they work together, go ahead and skip the next couple of paragraphs. If you do not, I hope you find this necessarily cursory explanation helpful.

---

20. For a book that makes this point in a most compelling way, see Dean, *Almost Christian*.

21. I offer two suggestions, but hasten to say that many exist. First, J. Ellsworth Kalas's *Christian Believer* is a good place to start. Second is McGrath, *Theology*. In a little more than 150 pages, McGrath introduces readers to the basic questions of the Christian faith addressed by the categories of systematic theology. It includes a glossary.

The word *theology* gets used two basic ways. It refers to the study of theology as a whole, but it also designates the narrow category of the doctrine of God. Thus under this umbrella term, theologians explore material associated with God's attributes, like love and holiness. The mysterious doctrine of the Trinity fits here as well, and many other questions about God's nature and purposes.

"Anthropology" in Christian theology has to do with two concerns: human nature as God created it and "the human problem," or the mystery of sin. Here students of theology will encounter the concept of being created in God's image, for example. The nature and impact of sin on human life is explored as well. Reflecting on the paradox and tension between the goodness of God's creation seen in humans *and* the horror associated with sin prompts deeply important questions that cause us to wrestle with faith. It is why I spoke earlier to the problem of seeing sin only in terms of rebellion and punishment and not in terms of imprisonment or disease. In turn, these thoughts help us see the relevance of considering what God does in view of human sin. Theology (the doctrine of God) and anthropology (the doctrine of human nature and condition) overlap and interact with each other, as do all the theological categories.

At this point we can start to see connections to other doctrines already covered in previous chapters. Christology examines teaching about who Jesus is and what he came to do. You can see how this material relates back both to theology and anthropology. We understand who Jesus is and what he has done on our behalf in light of what we know about God and what we realize about the human problem. Jesus' divinity not only points to God as Trinity, it reflects on what needs to be done to save us and who is capable of and qualified to accomplish this mission. Furthermore, as I have also already stated, Jesus as fully human person shows us God's full intention for human fulfillment.

The point about Jesus as Model and Exemplar urges us toward thinking about the meaning and purpose of the Christian life. This is the doctrinal category of soteriology, the doctrine of salvation or the Christian life. Like the others, it includes all manner of questions: what does it mean to be "saved," what is required for salvation, and so on. It touches on matters like the role of faith, the purpose of baptism, or the nature of repentance. It integrates with Christology by challenging us to think about how the character of Jesus teaches about who we are as disciples.

Ecclesiology has to do with teachings about the church, so, in that sense, it addresses the corporate dimension of the life of salvation. As we already noted, this doctrine touches on questions about how to identify the true church and what functions the church undertakes. It prompts questions about mission and how the church as a whole embodies God's work in history. Again we see how the various categories of systematic theology interact and loop back on each other, since, in doing work on the doctrine of the church, we engage matters of theology (narrowly understood, see paragraph above) and Christology.

Finally, we come to eschatology, the study of last things. Again, as we have pointed out, this category touches not only on end times and the fulfillment of biblical prophecy. It speaks to God's ultimate purposes and how they are fulfilled. It explores topics like the new creation and questions of final destiny, of heaven and hell. In truth, we cannot talk about eschatology without looking at all the other categories. For example, the characteristics of the Christian life (soteriology) speak to God's purposes with regard to spiritual gifts for ministry, while the doctrine of the church (ecclesiology) engages the same concerns.

If we want to grow to maturity, we must interact with ideas rooted in each of these categories. It does not mean, of course, that we must become systematic theologians in the academic sense. It does mean that there is a more-than-academic reason for this vast material. Again I appeal to the reader to remember the integrated, three-dimensional nature of the heart. Making the commitment to grow requires that we engage teachings that affect far more than just our ideas.

I could offer many examples to illustrate my claim, but let me try this one. You probably have heard the saying (notice how doctrine creeps in), "There are no bad people, only bad choices and bad actions." I appreciate the sentiment and think I understand its intent, which I will not bother to summarize now. Let us practice some doctrinal thinking and see how practical the work turns out to be. With regard to "no bad people," we can think of two important truths: human beings are created in God's image (therefore good), and we are also subject to sin (therefore bad, in terms of not hitting the mark God intends for us). Immediately we can see that the statement is too simplistic. It captures a portion of the truth. Half-truths are almost always far more dangerous than open untruths.

Doing what looks like the simple intellectual work of analysis begins to render more practical questions. What, for example, might we be trying to protect by saying that there are no bad people, only good people making bad choices? What does the statement suggest that we care about, if we believe it? Furthermore, what does the word *choices* suggest? Can we make choices as freely as this slogan seems to imply?

This doctrine masquerading as a slogan makes a claim about the human condition that puts distance between evil and human nature. Maybe I am reading into it more than I should but even so, it works as a thought experiment to illustrate the formative power of doctrine. What if a Christian really believes that we're not bad people, but good people making bad choices? What does it suggest about sin? Does it adequately explain the power of sin? Do I really have the freedom to make choices in the manner that the slogan seems to suggest? If I sometimes freely make bad choices can I just as freely make good ones? What about all the mixed motives and competing desires that I *feel*? And if this slogan accurately reflects the way we humans are, what does it suggest about Christ's death on the cross? Did Jesus die just to help me learn to stop making bad choices and start making good ones? Why did he need to die to teach me that?

Remember, doctrine teaches us what to care about and, in turn, shapes our dispositions over time. So, what does the statement teach me to care about? Well, I can learn to ignore those feelings of shame or guilt, because I now realize that I'm a good person. If I learn to pay attention to the choices I make and work hard to make sure they're always good choices, then life should go pretty well for me. I also likely will become wary and even suspicious toward any teaching that seems to support anything less than the freedom I believe I have with regard to choice. Doctrine does teach us what to care about. It significantly shapes how we will act under certain conditions even when we are virtually unaware of the specific teaching that may be driving our emotionally tonal thoughts and actions.

How would people assess themselves on the question of doctrine, then? Recognizing once more the many entry points into this task, I offer a few starting suggestions. First, people need to learn what the categories of theology are and why they matter to life (not just to ideas). We do not need to use all the technical terms, but it certainly does not hurt people to know their basic definitions. Vocabulary is like a toolbox: the more tools you have, the more equipped you are to do the job. More importantly, people need to know how to explore materials associated with the categories, even if they prefer not to use the technical language.

One way this happens already in some churches is that membership classes touch on most or all of these themes as preparation to join the church. Much more needs to be done, however. People responsible for teaching, from academicians to Sunday school teachers and small group leaders, need to know the broad outlines of theology and how to communicate them to people they teach.[22] Most importantly, teachers should repeatedly show people *why* the doctrines matter by connecting via illustrations and stories to real-life situations. We who are teachers need to teach people, so to speak, what God cares about so that we can know also what to care about.

Pastoral leaders can and should use the divisions of systematic theology to think strategically about sermon themes and classes to offer, but they should also strive to connect the same concerns to the experiences people have. I am speaking about youth and young people as well as older adults and even, to some degree, small children. For example, when people are planning a mission trip, how can they optimize the experience by connecting what the participants will be seeing and doing to relevant theological questions? The sky is truly the limit here. There is no single-source manual that teaches us how to proceed. It calls for experimentation, which itself is part of the journey of growth.

I suggest using the trajectory from chapter 2 again to help those in leadership positions think about how to organize the work of doctrinal instruction. With each area of the trajectory, leaders can ask questions about the various divisions of systematic theology. For example, we could ask, "Knowing what we know of God's nature, how do we see God at work in someone who is asleep?" (Or awakened, or stepping over the threshold into faith, etc.) Incorporating serious and sustained attempts to help people interact with the church's doctrines will produce the fruit of spiritual maturity if undertaken in concert with the goal of self-awareness.

PRACTICES (MEANS OF GRACE)

With what we have put in place above, we can now turn to the lists that people make to help them gauge spiritual health. They go by differing

---

22. The importance of this work comes through in the comment in James about not many people being teachers. See Jas 3:1ff.

names with "spiritual disciplines" the most common. I want to add the idea, taken from John Wesley's language, that they are means of grace, with emphasis on the word *means*. The practices themselves have value, but at least in terms of the aims of this book, they are means, not ends in themselves. Remember, grace is God's activity. The means of grace, therefore are ways in which God works in our hearts to stimulate growth.[23] The end is spiritual maturity, living into the measure of the full stature of Christ. If our practices do not compel us in this direction, something is fundamentally broken in our understanding of the practices.

Roughly thirty years ago, Richard Foster reintroduced a generation of Christians to the spiritual disciplines, and I still think his book, *Celebration of Discipline*, is one of the best.[24] It divides into three parts: (1) The Inward Disciplines, (2) The Outward Disciplines, and (3) the Corporate Disciplines. Part 2 includes an important chapter on service, so there we can see that disciplines involve more than just inward behaviors. Part 3 includes worship, also not typically understood in terms of spiritual disciplines. Anyone wishing a substantial overview of the spiritual disciplines will find this book well worth the time. I recommend it enthusiastically. Let us consider a few of these core practices.

Worship

Years ago, when our four children were school-age and we were hauling them off to worship every Sunday, I remember struggling with explaining to them why "going to church" was not a decision that we made week to week. As pastor, I had had many conversations with parents struggling to land upon a workable resolution of the constant battle with kids not wanting to go to church. Nobody likes going through the same argument

---

23. For the interested reader, two books by the same author explain Wesley's contribution and guidance on this important topic. See Knight, *Eight Life-Enriching Practices of United Methodists*. The reference to United Methodists in the title should not deter the reader. Although the book might be hard to find, for a more detailed exploration of John Wesley's understanding of the means of grace, see Knight, *The Presence of God in the Christian Life*. This book is academic in the best sense of that term. For the interested, nonexpert reader, it offers challenging but very rewarding reading.

24. Foster, *Celebration of Discipline*. Of course, he has written several important books since then, including his 1992 work, *Prayer*. I would also add the works of Dallas Willard for modern, contemporary writers who address important topics in substantial yet accessible ways. See his *The Spirit of the Disciplines*.

every Sunday morning, as children protest having to sit through another boring worship service.

With our children, I decided to take the straightforward path. "Yes," I admitted to my kids, church unfortunately is often boring for children (and adults). I told my kids that it was OK to feel bored. I am a preacher's kid. I went to church every Sunday, and I also went to Sunday evening church and Wednesday night prayer meeting. Because my father served small, rural congregations, I was often the only kid in the building. I remember feeling bored beyond description, thinking that Dad's thirty-minute sermon took an eternity. So now, as a pastor, I admitted to my kids that church can be very boring. Their complaint granted, the main reason we go to church is to honor God and to tell the story of what God has done on our behalf in Christ. It thus didn't really matter if we feel bored or not. They didn't argue, perhaps in part because they knew Mom and Dad wouldn't budge anyway. But I want to believe that it made sense to them.

"Worship" in its basic definition means to declare the value or worth of an object. Christian worship happens when people gather to declare the glory and goodness of God. It is of fundamental importance that we keep this point firmly in mind. It is the ruling assumption that puts into perspective all the fussing and shifting around that we American Protestants are prone to do these days. Some years ago, worship leader Matt Redman wrote, "I'm coming back to the heart of worship and it's all about you, Jesus."[25] The song became a big hit among churches and groups that do "contemporary"[26] worship. Ironically, we sing, "It's all about you, Jesus," and then we fight about what songs to sing, what instruments to play, what kind of content to cover in the sermon, and so on. People leave one church and try another until they find their particular predilections satisfied. Too often, it's all about us.

Worship, understood as a means of grace, completely reverses this direction. Worship demands that we bow to the supreme Presence, the ultimate Authority, the Majestic Glory. We worship because *we are created* to worship. The triune God is the ultimate object of our affection. Practicing this truth, we begin to discover, over time, that *we are changing*. Our interests, concerns, desires, and values all change, slowly, slowly, God-ward. God's thoughts, as it were, imbue ours, and we begin to care

25. Redman, "Heart of Worship."

26. I put the term in quotes because it has become a bone of contention among various groups concerned about worship in our time.

about what God cares about. How does this change happen? Grace: the action of the Holy Spirit.

Bible Reading

Sadly, most Christians do not know how to study the Bible. You may be one of the exceptions or you know some exceptions. I hope so. In my experience, however, Christians make two major mistakes in reading the Scriptures, which undercuts scriptural wisdom. First, they read the Bible only devotionally, which means in exceedingly small portions and for sometimes the wrong purpose, to find that word that "applies" to their lives.[27] I shall never forget a student from earlier in my career who often included in his papers the phrase, "how it relates to my life." If he could not see quickly how a required book related to his life, he dismissed it as unimportant. Preachers can compound this problem sometimes by the way we preach. We desperately want the word to be relevant to people's lives. We want them to grow (but we also don't want to bore them), so we emphasize the "practical," but I have begun to think that a near obsession with the practical or experiential often turns out to be premature, in fact, peremptory of the larger work the Holy Spirit does in us. "Practical" often results in superficial, cliché, repetitious, experiences that distort (by ignoring) other facets of discipleship that would lead us into maturity. Here we could circle back to the section on doctrine for fruitful reflection about the negative impact of emphasizing "practical" and ignoring "doctrinal."

Rather than moving so hastily to the practical application, we should slow down and listen, for *what the Bible tells us* is important. It means we need to practice attending to the actual wording of the text without moving too quickly to conclusions. A three-step process in inductive Bible study that people have followed uses these three terms: (1) observation, (2) interpretation, and (3) application. I like this pattern. Observation means working to notice as many of the features of the text under study as one can. It requires reading passages in context. Sometimes the observations have to do with structural features, as in the literary style (poetic or prose, for example) or when one notices a word or idea repeated or an

---

27. If I am searching the Bible for what applies to my life, who stays in control of the process?

odd break in the narrative flow. Sometimes observation has to do with ideas or claims or arguments.

Sometimes, with observation, it seems like we're stating the obvious, even repeating verbatim what the text under examination says. But this step cannot be skipped or taken too lightly. We must *slow down* to notice what is actually in the text. When we slow down and force ourselves to pay attention to the actual words on the page, the Spirit begins to whisper to us, causing us to notice what we have not noticed before and helping us to see how often we impose our already-worked-out conclusions onto the text. Observation is simply trying to see what is *there* before asking the question, What does it mean? The meaning question is the next step of interpretation. Far too often people rush to the What does it mean? question without having adequately looked at what is actually in the text.[28]

A significant facet of the interpretive task involves asking reflective questions without worrying too much up front if those questions render tight, coherent answers. More reflection can modify and hone one's thoughts. Reflecting on the text without feeling the need to come up with an answer all the time is itself a means of grace. Mysteriously, over time, confidence in the Scriptures increases even when one does not find satisfying answers to immediate questions. Often, other unexpected insights surface. Other pieces fall into place. If we hurry through the Bible reading, or only read in tiny portions, we are unlikely to have the experience that comes from this depth of reading the Bible.[29]

Coupled with the need to slow the pace of Bible study is the need for reading long sections in one sitting. John Wesley called it "searching the Scriptures." That word *searching* is very important. It suggests time, effort, and intensity. It speaks about desire. When one searches for something, one's heart is in the search. Far too many times have I sat with students who only read the Bible devotionally. Even though they revere the Bible, its truths actually remain secondary to the nuggets of personal well-being students seek. Neither does listening to sermons every week, even if the

28. A well-known inductive Bible study guide is Arthur, *How to Study Your Bible*. I admit to some mixed feelings about the book, but I think she does an excellent job of showing the importance of distinguishing and following the steps that I've mentioned, and she gives very useful tips on how to organize one's study.

29. The process I am describing requires no "professional" skill or training in Bible reading. It only requires the willingness to take the time to attend to the texture and terrain of the biblical writings.

preacher is the greatest Bible expositor in the world, produce mature Christians. There is no substitute for engaging the Scriptures in big doses.

One of the saddest moments in my ministry as a pastor was discovering this bad habit in a group of my congregants. I was their new young pastor and learned that a group of them had been gathering for years once a week for Bible study. I was excited and asked to join them. They willingly agreed. I attended the next meeting and witnessed one of the saddest displays of confusion and lack of productive conversation I think I had ever seen. They literally took turns reading one verse at a time. A person would read the verse and then, for a few minutes, the group would discuss what they thought the verse meant. They expressed hesitance. They speculated. They guessed. And then they went on to the next verse. Each segment of conversation related to the verse seemed completely disconnected from the previous one. I wanted to cry. These dear brothers and sisters—many years my senior, who should have been wise in the faith—had given years and years of time and effort to Bible study to almost no avail.

The only solution to this problem is to give ample time to pore over the text in large chunks. Let all the questions bubble to the surface. Don't try to eat the elephant all at once. Write down your questions, fragmented thoughts, and insights. Read and discuss with other people. Group Bible study that keeps members clear about the purpose of Bible study (to grow to maturity and to engage more lovingly in mission) helps foster the corporate sense of maturity. Check written resources (but be careful about the public domain stuff online!). Ask not only your pastor but also people you know who demonstrate biblical wisdom, whose lives show the fruit of time spent in the Word. Quiz them about the study helps and other sources that have provoked growth in them. And stick with the practice for the long haul.

If people follow some practice such as I am advocating (and if they avoid the bad habits I've complained about), they will discover, as with worship, that something happens in them. Especially with Bible study we find a paradox: we discover how many questions we have and how many lack a definitive answer, but we also discover which questions are really important and which don't need that lock-down conclusion.[30] We

---

30. I do not mean to suggest that we get sloppy or relativistic in our search for truth. I am talking about wisdom to know the difference between questions that need definitive answers and those that do not.

find ourselves growing in, for lack of a better term, spiritual confidence, a sense and perspective about life that helps one feel settled and steady, even when circumstances are not. Spiritual confidence is not the same as academic acumen, but not opposed to it. Intellectual knowledge may help us master concepts, but searching the Scriptures, as a means of grace, is much deeper, more personal, and more whole-person than academic study usually involves.

Even more so than with the topic of worship, I appeal to non-ordained, non-professional people on this point about Bible study. Survey after survey, from Gallup to Barna (polling organizations), has shown the dearth of Bible knowledge. Illiterate people in earlier generations knew the Bible better than many of us today, even though we can read and have such easy access to the Scriptures. Our non-reading ancestors soaked up the Scriptures through listening to others read, through singing the Scriptures in hymns, through connecting visual images on church buildings and in stained glass and icons and paintings to the Bible stories they heard. Truly, one of the most embarrassing features of modern Christian life is our ignorance of the Bible.

At the risk of annoyance, I remind the reader again that practicing self-awareness while reading the Bible, individually and in groups, makes the practice the most salutary. With humility we open ourselves to the Spirit's work to shape us according to the character of Christ.

Prayer

I stand in awe of "prayer warriors," as they are sometimes called. I've been privileged to know a number of them—people who spend long hours in prayer, especially intercessory prayer, who seem to have honed the ability of prevailing upon the Lord. They bear visible fruit. They are wise, peaceful, faithful, effective witnesses to the Gospel. Although I pray daily, I do not count myself among them. For some, prayer feels like a chore rather than a joy, yet prayer is as vital to our growth toward maturity as it is to those who truly love to pray.

As with other topics in the Christian life, we often get trapped in well-worn but unfruitful debates. How and in what manner does God answer prayer? When we pray for sick people, does God ever heal by means beyond natural bodily processes or the usual medical interventions? Can we "change God's mind" by praying? If God already knows what we need before we ask, why do we ask? What happens to people's faith if they pray for something and it doesn't happen? I will not try to answer any of these questions.

Rather, I wish to focus on three somewhat unrelated points that I believe help clarify how prayer is a means of grace. They have to do with listening as much as talking, with praying candidly—that is, praying what we actually feel and telling God these things in unvarnished language—and, finally, about the value of including formal, written prayers (especially of the great saints) among our extemporaneous private prayers.

First is listening in prayer. I do think that most of us spend most of the time in prayer talking and expressing our heart's desires to the Lord. This habit is completely appropriate. I pray daily for my children, for the campus where I work, for my co-workers, for the Kingdom to come. I do lots of talking in prayer. But listening is truly as important and is the dimension of prayer we most easily overlook, which relates to why I referred to Bible reading as like prayer. When we read the Bible prayerfully, openly, and attentively, when we invite God to speak to us and then take the time to listen, God actually speaks.

Listening to God, for most of us, requires some kind of action and structure. The picture of someone sitting in mystical posture, motionless, does not, I think, encourage many people to pray. It seems like one has to be a super saint to achieve this degree of stillness. Even if we can sit still physically, the monkeys in our minds continue to romp around with a thousand distracting thoughts. However, with structure, persistence, and practice, we can learn to listen. For example, some people journal in prayer. They write down thoughts as they surface. As long as the person praying attends to the Lord in prayer and governs the writing so that she or he is not just jotting notes, but actually writing from a sense of response to God's whisperings, then capturing thoughts by writing can be most helpful.

In one sense I am going against the grain with my suggestions about prayer because I am trying to place more emphasis on listening than talking. Furthermore, although the various acronyms[31] that people have devised for structuring their prayer lives are useful, I do think that we should spend more time in silence than talking. For one thing, we do not structure our conversations in other relationships this way. Imagine that

31. Many people know the ACTS acronym: adoration, confession, thanksgiving, supplication.

if every time I sat down with you to have a conversation, I went through the same exact steps. Would it feel like a relationship? I certainly don't want anyone to stop using his or her patterns in prayer, but I think more time for listening allows an actual relationship with God to develop.

So much for listening in prayer. The second point to consider has to do with candidness. We should pray openly, expressing our raw feelings to God. Because worship and other forms of church practices have loosened and become more informal over the past thirty to forty years, perhaps the stilted, formal, "religious" language often used in prayer has also waned. I think, however, that the problem of people feeling hesitant about what to say in prayer persists. As with so many other aspects of life, we ordained preachers have professionalized prayer and our folk have gone along with us. I have a hunch that, because so many people feel hesitant to pray in public for lack of knowing "the right words," it affects private prayer as well.

For this reason, I love praying the psalms. Occasionally, when someone comes with a personal struggle, I will suggest praying the words of specific psalms. I almost always include Ps 22, because it starts with the words that Jesus prayed from the cross: "My God, my God, why have you forsaken me?" If you look at the psalms of lament (complaint), you see that unvarnished, raw, open quality of the language. The psalmist is not afraid to express exactly what is on his mind: "God, have you forgotten me? Do you even care? Are you asleep? Should I even trust you?" But notice, also, the turn that happens in virtually all of these songs of complaint. The psalmist begins by expressing in strong terms his anguish, but ends with, "the poor shall eat and be satisfied," that "all the families of the nations will worship before the Lord" and that future generations, too, will know the Lord's goodness. Lament turns to praise.

I think we see in the pattern of these psalms a big lesson on grace in prayer. When we are bold enough to express without reservation the contents of our feelings to God, then God works in a special way. The transparency of feeling is salutary *for us*. God knows the true contents of our hearts. Getting to that degree of candor opens us to the work of God in our lives. I believe this point holds especially true for the deep, lurking doubts, so troubling that we fear actually expressing them. Yet, when we do, God faithfully and graciously answers. As we develop openness to express all the contents of our hearts, God answers with grace and we grow. We draw closer to the vision of maturity found in the Scriptures.

Now let's explore the other side of the coin. I just talked about candidness in prayer and now I want to advocate for using someone else's prayers. I am thinking of the great saints of the church over the years, like St. Augustine or John of the Cross or Teresa of Avila or John Wesley or E. Stanley Jones. It seems, therefore, as if I am contradicting what I just said, but I don't think so. What often seems like candidness in our extemporaneous prayers in actuality reveals the well-worn ruts of our prayers, exposing as well the numbing *pro forma* quality that can afflict extemporaneous prayer. We also can become very self-absorbed in our prayers. For both reasons, praying the published words of an exemplary Christian or of the church's liturgy offers the practical benefit of "listening" to someone else in prayer. It can broaden our vision and open our hearts to growth. Ironically, most of the time, listening to our contemporaries pray—in a prayer meeting, for example—does not have this effect. When we gather to pray we often focus on intercessory prayer, which we all know is only one part of prayer. The great saints and liturgies teach us to pray. They add richness. With the vast online sources available, one can find a sampling of these prayers rather easily.

Service/Ministry

I still remember the first time I read John Wesley's sermon, "On Visiting the Sick." In the opening paragraphs, he states that we usually think of the means of grace as coming only through such practices as the Lord's Supper. Wesley, however, argues forcefully that "works of mercy," as he called them, also are channels of grace. God works in the one(s) giving the ministry as well as the one(s) receiving it. In the case of visiting the sick, therefore, God works in the *visitor's life* as that person engages in ministry, as well as the one who receives the visit.[32]

Many people, when stopping to think of it, recognize Wesley's point. How many times have you heard someone mention (or said yourself) how good it feels to serve other people, even though we find it hard to schedule the time and break away from the normal routine. That "feeling good" hints at the work that God does in our hearts when we engage in

---

32. In print, this sermon can be found in two editions of Wesley's *Works*. In the 1986 Baker reprint, see volume 7 (Sermons, vol. 3), 117–27. In the Abingdon Bicentennial Edition, see volume 3, 385–97. For an online version, see http://gbgm-umc.org/umhistory/wesley/sermons.

ministry. What we know intuitively, we should make more explicit and central to our lives.

In other words, ministry should be a regular aspect of life for every Christian, a normal feature of what we do. Thinking about our motives is particularly important on this point. Most of the people I know are extremely busy, responsible people. They take leadership roles in all kinds of church and community organizations. The same holds for college students. In addition to coursework, papers and projects, they lead campus organizations. Even when we engage in "service," we tend to find ways to fit it into tightly managed schedules in an ad hoc way.

Tucking little bits of service here and there does not adequately get at the Bible's call for us to engage in ministry. It does not mean that we all do the same kind of ministry. It does mean that we ask questions about God's claim and call, which requires the openness and humility of self-awareness. A few people have made service a characteristic of their life. Talking to these folks, one begins to see how big an impact ministry has had on them. They are talented, gifted people who could be doing all sorts of things, but they have made disciplined, strategic choices in order to concentrate on some ministry that grips their hearts.

I have been in ordained ministry my entire adult life, except for a brief stint at public school teaching. I have watched and tried to emulate leading pastors and professors over the years, but I am most moved by the regular Christian laypeople who work hard at their jobs, take care of their families *and* provide exemplary ministry leadership, often at significant cost to their personal time and financial situations. As I write these words, I'm thinking of two friends who, for years, have led a prison ministry. I know their stories fairly well. Neither set out early in life to get into this work, but they heard God's call and they answered. Their experience illustrates how the call can come incrementally, often in ways that we do not initially recognize as God's call. God knows just the right time to challenge us to take the next step and these two friends have done exactly that. They have developed an after care ministry for men who have served their time in prison and who need help successfully reentering life outside the prison walls. I have had the privilege of knowing some of these former inmates, brothers in Christ, who are growing and thriving because of the spiritual leadership of two men willing to be used by God.

To be sure, these friends have had their hearts broken by taking risks inherent in ministry. Not every person they have tried to help has stayed with the after care program. There have been, if not failures ("failure" is much too final a word when God is involved), certainly moments of discouragement as they have watched men in whom they have poured their lives turn away from the help extended them. Real ministry always involves exposing oneself to the suffering that Christ felt for the world. Paul prayed that he would know Christ and the power of his resurrection, but also *the fellowship of his suffering*. We are blinded by the myth of success in this country. When we engage in the kind of ministry that reflects Christ's redemptive purposes, we will suffer heartache. We will be occasionally discouraged and our faith will be tested.

And all that, too, is a means of grace. If ever we can see a manifestation of God's sovereignty, it emerges here, as we share the sufferings of Jesus.[33] God takes the most painful of circumstances, in which we have stuck our necks and hearts out to others only to have our love rebuffed or misunderstood in some way, and turns the pain we experience into growth for us. God deepens our understanding while healing our wounds. Ministry that involves our hearts is always risky. Facing this reality calls for courage and persistence. It challenges our faith and tests our commitment. All of the messiness and risk of ministry falls within God's grace. God can take all of it to accomplish his redemptive purposes, both for us and for the world. This perspective may seem too idealistic or unrealistic, but I am convinced that the Bible unrelentingly presents exactly this vision.

PRACTICE ALL THREE

Imagine belonging to a body of believers committed to the totality of what we have covered in this chapter. Together they agree to work at gaining appropriate self-awareness. They open themselves not only to their own internal thoughts, but to others. They live transparent lives. They practice speaking the truth to one another in love so that all can come to maturity.[34] This means that they learn how to talk and listen to one another, staying committed to the Body even when conflict and trouble arise. They undertake the hard work of doctrinal formation, knowing that doctrine shapes what they care about, knowing also that it will help them care about what God cares about. The work of self-awareness and doctrinal

33. See Phil 3:10.
34. Eph 4:15.

formation shows up in the way they actually live, especially in the sacrificial ministries they do for others. Imagine this spiritually mature church.

Is the vision simply too much to ask? Is it too hard, too idealistic? If you were to look back over the topics we have covered in this book, you would see that I am convinced that the answer is no. Not only is this vision not impossibly idealistic, *God commands it.* The Scriptures teach it. To paraphrase St. Augustine's prayer in his *Confessions,* God gives what God commands. John Wesley believed that God's grace turns God's commands into promises. The imperative moves to the indicative. What God has told us to be and do, God will through grace enable us to be and do.

When it comes to assessing growth, we must include the three dimensions covered in this chapter. I admit that I, too, have therefore given you a list to follow, a list with three categories. I have employed a number of terms throughout this book to speak to the complex workings of the heart, but maybe, in the end, we can settle on these three: *doctrines, dispositions,* and *disciplines.* Over the years Christians have paid attention to all three, in varying degrees, with varying emphases (depending on the concerns found within particular historical and cultural contexts). I have been arguing that, to grow to maturity, we need always to keep in mind all three dimensions and to pay particular attention to how they interact with one another. They reveal the very inner workings of the heart.

There is much more that I wish to say and a few things about which I worry, out of fear that I have not made some things clear. Especially in talking about emotions and dispositions, for example, I wish I had time to explain how disposition does not mean the same as personality. Although I have used a number of personality[35] instruments to learn about myself and have suggested them to others, I hope we will not confuse disposition with personality. God and the experiences of my upbringing (in other words, God) have given me a unique personality. Personality is part of what makes us individual beings. But I have used disposition to point to that combination of thoughts, feelings, desires, and motives that produce actions commensurate with the character of Christ. Even though we have individual personalities, we want to make visible the nature and purposes of Christ.

---

35. By personality inventories I mean such instruments as the Myers-Briggs Personality Type Indicator or the Birkman Scale or even the StrengthsQuest instrument devised by the Gallup organization and used widely on college campuses.

In the end, for spiritual maturity, Christ embodies the standard. Yes, it is a daunting prospect, this call to look like our Lord. Thus, we conclude with this thought from Phil 3:12–15a: "Not that I have already obtained it or have already reached the goal; but I press on to make it my own, because Christ Jesus has made me his own. Beloved, I do not consider that I have made it my own; but this one thing I do: forgetting what lies behind and straining forward to what lies ahead, I press on toward the goal for the prize of the heavenly call of God in Christ Jesus. Let those of us then who are mature be of the same mind." Press on, friends. Press on.

Bibliography

Abraham, William J. *Aldersgate and Athens: John Wesley and the Foundations of Christian Belief.* Waco: Baylor University Press, 2010.
———. *Crossing the Threshold of Divine Revelation.* Grand Rapids: Eerdmans, 2006.
Arendt, Hannah. *The Life of the Mind: The Groundbreaking Investigation on How We Think.* San Diego: Harcourt, 1978.
Arthur, Kay. *How to Study Your Bible: The Lasting Rewards of the Inductive Approach.* Eugene, OR: Harvest House, 1994.
Augustine. *The Confessions of St. Augustine.* Translated by John Kenneth Ryan. Garden City, NY: Image, 1960.
Bainton, Roland. *Here I Stand: A Life of Martin Luther.* New York: New American Library, 1950.
Barclay, William. *The Letters to the Philippians, Colossians, and Thessalonians.* Rev. ed. Daily Study Bible Series. Philadelphia: Westminster, 1975.
Barna Group. "Many Churchgoers and Faith Leaders Struggle to Define Spirituality." Online: http://www.barna.org/barna-update/article/12-faithspirituality.
Betz, Hans Dieter. *The Sermon on the Mount: A Commentary on the Sermon on the Mount, Including the Sermon on the Plain (Matthew 5:3—7:27 and Luke 6:20–49).* Hermeneia: A Critical and Historical Commentary on the Bible. Minneapolis: Fortress, 1995.
Boyatzis, Richard, and Annie McKee. *Resonant Leadership: Renewing Yourself and Connecting with Others through Mindfulness, Hope, and Compassion.* Boston: Harvard Business School Press, 2005.
Brown, Francis, S. R. Driver, and Charles A. Briggs. *The Brown-Driver-Briggs Hebrew and English Lexicon.* Peabody, MA: Hendrickson, 2001.
Brueggemann, Walter. *Theology of the Old Testament: Testimony, Dispute, Advocacy.* Minneapolis: Fortress, 1997.
Brun, Georg, Ulvi Doğuoğlu, and Dominique Kuenzle, editors. *Epistemology and Emotions.* Burlington, VT: Ashgate, 2008.
Calvin, John. *On the Christian Life.* Online: http://www.ccel.org/ccel/calvin/chr_life.iii.html.
Card, Michael. "Joy in the Journey." From the album *The Final Word.* Sparrow Records, 1987. Online: http://michaelcard.com/timeline.html.
Clapper, Gregory. *As if the Heart Mattered: A Wesleyan Spirituality.* Nashville: Upper Room, 1997.

————. *John Wesley on Religious Affections: His View on Experience and Emotion and Their Role in the Christian Life and Theology*. Metuchen, NJ: Scarecrow, 1989.

Covey, Stephen M. R. *The Speed of Trust: The One Thing that Changes Everything*. New York: Free Press, 2006.

Dean, Kenda Creasy. *Almost Christian: What the Faith of Our Teenagers Is Telling the American Church*. New York: Oxford University Press, 2010.

Dixon, Thomas. *From Passions to Emotions: The Creation of a Secular Psychological Category*. Cambridge: Cambridge University Press, 2003.

Edwards, Jonathan. *The Religious Affections*. Carlisle, PA: Banner of Truth, 1961.

Evans, Dylan. *The Science of Sentiment*. Oxford: Oxford University Press, 2001.

Fitzmyer, Joseph A. *First Corinthians*. The Anchor Yale Bible 32. New Haven: Yale University Press, 2008.

Foster, Richard J. *Celebration of Discipline: The Paths to Spiritual Growth*. San Francisco: Harper & Row, 1978.

————. *Prayer: Finding the Heart's True Home*. New York: HarperOne, 1992.

Freedman, David Noel. *The Anchor Bible Dictionary*. 6 vols. New York: Doubleday, 1992.

Goleman, Daniel. *Emotional Intelligence: Why It Can Matter More than IQ*. New York: Bantam, 1995.

————. *Social Intelligence: The Revolutionary New Science of Human Relationships*. New York: Bantam, 2006.

Goleman, Daniel, Richard Boyatzis, and Annie McKee. *Primal Leadership: Realizing the Power of Emotional Intelligence*. Boston: Harvard Business School Press, 2002.

Grenz, Stanley J. *The Millennial Maze: Sorting Out Evangelical Options*. Downers Grove, IL: InterVarsity, 1992.

Griffiths, Paul E. *What Emotions Really Are: The Problem of Psychological Categories*. Chicago: University of Chicago Press, 1997.

Hagee, John. *Jerusalem Countdown*. Lake Mary, FL: Frontline, 2006.

Helm, Bennet. *Emotional Reason: Deliberation, Motivation, and the Nature of Value*. Cambridge: Cambridge University Press, 2003.

Henderson, D. Michael. *John Wesley's Class Meeting: A Model for Making Disciples*. Nappanee, IN: Evangel, 1997.

Hoehner, Harold W. *Ephesians: An Exegetical Commentary*. Grand Rapids: Baker, 2002.

Hunter, James Davison. *To Change the World: The Irony, Tragedy, and Possibility of Christianity in the Late Modern World*. New York: Oxford University Press, 2010.

Irenaeus. *Against Heresies*. In *Ante-Nicene Fathers*. Vol. 1, *The Apostolic Fathers, Justin Martyr, Irenaeus*. Edited by Alexander Roberts and James Donaldson. Revised and arranged by A. Cleveland Coxe. Peabody, MA: Hendrickson, 1994.

Kalas, J. Ellsworth. *Christian Believer: Knowing God with Heart and Mind*. Nashville: Abingdon, 1999.

Kiley, Dan. *The Peter Pan Syndrome: Men Who Have Never Grown Up*. New York: Dodd, Mead, 1983.

Kimball, Dan. *They Like Jesus but Not the Church: Insights from Emerging Generations*. Grand Rapids: Zondervan, 2007.

Kinnaman, David, and Gabe Lyons. *UnChristian: What a New Generation Really Thinks about Christianity . . . and Why It Matters*. Grand Rapids: Baker, 2007.

Kittel, Gerhard, editor. *Theological Dictionary of the New Testament*. 10 vols. Translated by Geoffrey W. Bromiley. Grand Rapids: Eerdmans, 1964.

Knight, Henry H. *Eight Life-Enriching Practices of United Methodists*. Nashville: Abingdon, 2001.

———, editor. *From Aldersgate to Azusa Street: Wesleyan, Holiness, and Pentecostal Visions of the New Creation*. Eugene, OR: Pickwick, 2010.

———. *The Presence of God in the Christian Life: John Wesley and the Means of Grace*. Pietist and Wesleyan Studies 3. Lanham, MD: Scarecrow, 1992.

Kouzes, James M., and Barry Z. Posner. *Christian Reflections on the Leadership Challenge*. San Francisco: Jossey-Bass, 2004.

———. *The Leadership Challenge*. San Francisco: Jossey-Bass, 2007.

Latourette, Kenneth Scott. *Christianity through the Ages*. New York: Harper & Row, 1965.

Lincoln, Andrew T. *Ephesians*. Word Biblical Commentary 42. Dallas: Word, 1990.

Maddox, Randy. *Responsible Grace: John Wesley's Practical Theology*. Nashville: Kingswood, 1994.

McGrath, Alister. *Theology: The Basics*. Malden, MA: Blackwell, 2004.

Nussbaum, Martha. *Upheavals of Thought: The Intelligence of Emotions*. Cambridge: Cambridge University Press, 2001.

Patterson, Kerry, Joseph Grenny, Ron McMillan, and Al Switzler. *Crucial Conversations: Tools for Talking when Stakes Are High*. New York: McGraw-Hill, 2002.

Plantinga, Alvin. *Warranted Christian Belief*. New York: Oxford University Press, 2000.

Plaut, W. Gunther. *The Torah: A Modern Commentary*. 3 vols. New York: Union of Hebrew Congregations, 1983.

Roberts, Robert C. *Spiritual Emotions: A Psychology of Christian Virtues*. Grand Rapids: Eerdmans, 2007.

Roof, Wade Clark. *A Generation of Seekers: The Spiritual Journeys of the Baby Boom Generation*. San Francisco: HarperCollins, 1994.

Sarna, Nahum. *Exploring Exodus: The Origins of Biblical Israel*. New York: Schocken, 1996.

Shoop, Robert J., Susan M. Scott, and Bill Snyder. *Leadership: Lessons from Bill Snyder*. Manhattan, KS: AG Press, 1998.

Stark, Rodney. *The Rise of Christianity: How the Obscure, Marginal Jesus Movement Became the Dominant Religious Force in the Western World in a Few Centuries*. San Francisco: HarperCollins, 1997.

Stein, K. James. *Philipp Jakob Spener: Pietist Patriarch*. Chicago: Covenant, 1986.

Telford, John, editor. *The Letters of the Rev. John Wesley*. 8 vols. London: Epworth, 1931.

Torrey, R. A., A. C. Dixon et al., editors. *The Fundamentals: A Testimony to the Truth*. 2 vols. 1917. Reprint, Grand Rapids: Baker, 2003.

Watson, Kevin M. *A Blueprint for Discipleship: Wesley's General Rules as a Guide to Christian Living*. Nashville: Discipleship Resources, 2009.

Wesley, Charles. "O for a Heart to Praise My God." In *The United Methodist Hymnal: Book of United Methodist Worship*, #417. Nashville: United Methodist Publishing House, 1989.

Wesley, John. "A Farther Appeal to Men of Reason and Religion," Part I. In *The Works of John Wesley*. Bicentennial ed. Edited by Albert C. Outler, 11:106. Nashville: Abingdon, 1986.

———. "On Working Out Our Own Salvation." In *The Works of John Wesley*. Bicentennial ed. Edited by Albert C. Outler, 3:199–209. Nashville: Abingdon, 1986.

———. "A Plain Account of Christian Perfection." In *The Works of John Wesley*. Edited by Thomas Jackson, 11:366–446. Grand Rapids: Baker, 1986.

————. "Preface to 1739 Hymns and Sacred Poems." In *The Works of John Wesley*. Edited by Thomas Jackson, 14:321. Grand Rapids: Baker, 1986.

————. "Preface to the Sermons." In *The Works of John Wesley*. Bicentennial ed. Edited by Albert C. Outler, 1:104–105. Nashville: Abingdon, 1984.

————. "Sermon on the Mount, IV." In *The Works of John Wesley*. Bicentennial ed. Edited by Albert C. Outler, 1:539. Nashville: Abingdon, 1984.

————. "The Witness of Our Own Spirit." In *The Works of John Wesley*. Bicentennial ed. Edited by Albert C. Outler, 1:309. Nashville: Abingdon, 1984.

————. *The Works of John Wesley*. 14 vols. Edited by Thomas Jackson. 1872. Reprint, Grand Rapids: Baker, 1978.

————. *The Works of John Wesley*. Bicentennial ed. 14 vols. Edited by Albert C. Outler. Nashville: Abingdon, 1984–.

Willard, Dallas. *The Spirit of the Disciplines: How God Changes Lives*. San Francisco: Harper & Row, 1988.